COME ABIDE

Come Abide
Con-solatio, a Ministry of Presence

(Stories of Genuine Friendship from Unexpected Places)

"The true measure of humanity is essentially determined in relationship to suffering and to the sufferer. This holds true both for the individual and for society. [. . .] To accept the 'other' who suffers, means that I take up his suffering in such a way that it becomes mine also. Because it has now become a shared suffering, though, in which another person is present, this suffering is penetrated by the light of love.

The Latin word con-solatio, 'consolation,' expresses this beautifully. It suggests being with the other in his solitude, so that it ceases to be solitude."

Encyclical Letter by Pope Benedict XVI - Spe Salvi #38

Meet Con-solatio

Con-solatio is a Brooklyn-based Catholic non-profit organization. It partners with other local non-profits in 18 different countries to run an international volunteer program. The volunteer program offers young adults ages 18–30 a unique opportunity to dedicate one to two years to serving those whom Christ loves the most: those who are lonely, forgotten, disabled, sick, imprisoned, orphaned, or elderly.

Our volunteers live in simple homes nestled in some of the world's most troubled areas in large cities. As a community of four to six international volunteers, we live alongside our neighbors—entering into their culture and lives. Each day is rooted in an intense prayer life including daily Mass, Rosary, Adoration, and Liturgy of the Hours. By spending time in God's company, we are then called to bring that Presence of hope to those who are suffering. We open our door to all those who knock, and we visit our friends both in our neighborhood and in places of greater suffering, such as prisons, hospitals, homeless shelters, and psychiatric wards. Our ministry of presence seeks to reveal the beauty and dignity of each person through a wide variety of activities and personal, life-transforming relationships.

Since Con-solatio's inception in 2005, over 120 young North Americans have experienced this life-changing opportunity— striving to offer a haven of love and peace to those whose hearts are wearied by loneliness and sorrow.

To learn more, visit us at www.con-solatio.org; follow us @consolatio.ministryofpresence on Instagram and Facebook; subscribe to our Youtube channel at Con-solatio; or email us at info@con-solatio.org.

Table of Contents

Foreword

"But then I met Con-solatio . . ." You will read this often in this book. "But then I met Con-solatio . . ."

In 2008, my family and I had recently moved to New York City because of a job I was offered as a theology professor at St. John's University. As my midwestern family put down roots here in New York City, I also began a website that shared some of my theological research on the spiritual writer Adrienne von Speyr, a laywoman, wife, mother, and physician whose writings have a deep influence on Con-solatio, as I came to learn. Members of the Con-solatio community reached out to me online, having seen my website on Adrienne and my new location in New York. They asked if we could meet to talk more about the spirituality of Adrienne and what it meant to be a young Catholic volunteer today. So it was that I first met Con-solatio: gathered around a small table with warm coffees, Italian cookies, and deep conversation.

In speaking with these members of Con-solatio, I began to realize that I was meeting a kind of incarnation of the spirituality of the woman Adrienne, whom I had spent so much time studying and writing about for others. To put it another way, I was meeting a living example of what it meant to be Mary at the Cross——a central image in Adrienne's spirituality. If there is one main takeaway I have from this book, it is this: that Con-solatio wants to be Mary at the Cross, to say "Yes" to Christ even there, to take Him into her heart even as He is abandoned. She alone does not leave Him alone.

As I came to learn more about this community, I discovered their daily consecration prayer that concludes with, "Yours is our family, Virgin Mary! We are yours!" In this prayer, they beg Mary to "Seal every one of our hearts with an immense compassion for every human being." I love this phrase—"an immense compassion." They pray daily to be "an immense compassion." What a way of holiness they have chosen! They pray to be overwhelming love to every person they encounter—the small, the weak, the forgotten, everyone that God sends to them.

As I read this book, I have been asking myself:

What happens when one says "Yes" to whatever God asks?

What does it mean to say "Yes" completely?

What happens when one says "Yes" to love itself?

The answer to these questions is in these young men and women of Con-solatio. Through the way that they live, I have come to see that to say "Yes" to others means to stand with them in every moment of their lives; to stand with them in their crosses and to stand with them in their resurrections. To say "Yes" means to be love as their lives touch the passion of Christ and the resurrection of Christ; to be with them in their darkness and their light. To say "Yes" means that I'm taking others into myself. I'm taking them into me as Mary is taking her son into her heart. Their sorrow is my sorrow. Their cross is my cross. And when their resurrection comes, their risen life is my risen life. Their joy is my joy.

By God's will, I have met many of these volunteers of Con-solatio whose stories you will read in this book. I also have met many other men and women who have been changed because they met Con-solatio. They speak about how Con-solatio gave them friendship, attention, and love to such an extent that their lives were changed from despair to hope, from loneliness to comfort, from sadness to joy. "But then they met Con-solatio . . ."

These men and women challenge me to give this unreserved "Yes" to God and to everyone He brings into my life. Like these volunteers, I also pray daily to be an immense compassion because I want to say "Yes" to God with nothing held back. By doing so, everything has changed in my own life. So, I ask you, what will happen when you say "Yes" to whatever God asks of you?

May Mary be with you as you read this book and may she help you say "Yes" like her, like Con-solatio.

— *Matthew Lewis Sutton, Ph.D., Associate Professor of Systematic Theology, St. John's University (NY)*

Introduction

A letter from Tegucigalpa, Honduras. In six dense pages of stories, faces, and encounters, Michael eagerly introduces Pedrito. Though he is a kid abandoned by his father and attacked by his neighbors, *"[h]e arrives at our home discreetly, makes sure no other child has followed him, and locks the door. 'Finally! The Con-solatio volunteers all to myself!' Behind his violence, there is a piercing cry: please love me!"*

A second letter from Salvador da Bahia, Brazil. In ecstatic jubilation, Claire writes the most surprising news, *"João, whom we deemed dead long ago, suddenly showed up out of nowhere." He speaks to us from his heart. He's contracted HIV and, in his early 20s, is condemned to leaving this life behind in a couple of months. 'I'm sorry for all I did! Will you please welcome me back? Can you walk the path with me? This is the only place where I have ever known love. I'm afraid to die alone.' The faces have changed. We volunteers who welcome João today are not the same who showed him love seven years ago. But it's the same home to his heart, the same abiding Presence."*

A third letter from Bangkok, Thailand. A 40th from Buenos Aires, Argentina. A 120th from Manila, Philippines. Thousands and thousands of dense, raw, consoling letters.

For years now, our hearts have burned with the certainty that these letters are teeming with flecks of the purest gold, found among the murkiest of muds. They are overflowing with a balm ready to be poured out on many wounds, to fill up the innermost crevices of our souls.

We, the members of Con-solatio, are now grateful and delighted to offer this humble book, which compiles excerpts of letters faithfully written by our North American volunteers in countries all around the world to their supporters.

The people to whom our volunteers will introduce you in these pages are our most valuable treasure. They have been our masters. At the school of their humble lives, we have learned how to love truly, to hope boldly, and to believe deeply. They have conferred on us, Con-solatio volunteers, the honor of calling them friends. By having been granted the undeserved grace of standing with them, in all of our own poverty, at the foot of their crosses, we have begun to understand Golgotha as the bridal bed where new life is conceived.

Journeying alongside our friends and volunteers, we have come face-to-face with a freeing truth: we cannot "save the world" by finding a solution to the "suffering of human beings." Suffering is not abstract. It burdens a very specific, unique heart–Kuya Julius', Rosa's, Pathamma's. It disfigures a very specific, unique face–Felipe's, Niña Rita's, Duwee's. We have come to learn that only a personal, abiding presence, standing next to a uniquely sorrowing heart can be, if not a solution, at least a sign of new life, a sign of hope.

In these pages, you are beginning a voyage.

The names of the volunteers are real. The loved ones they write about have been changed to protect their identity.

The itinerary is two-fold. Firstly, the journey is based on John 19:25, from where our ministry draws its deepest roots: *"Standing by the Cross of Jesus were his mother and his mother's sister, Mary the wife of Clopas, and Mary of Magdala . . . and the disciple whom he loved."*

Each chapter of this book invites you to join us in contemplating a different aspect sprung from this Bible verse. In Chapter One, we dive into the ultimate consequence of the Fiat: the total gift of self. In Chapter Two, we turn our gaze toward the Word—we listen to His cry and hear His silence. Chapter Three focuses on the need for others to stand by the Mother in this dark hour. Chapter Four leads us to meditate on Her *"com-patere"* (suffering alongside), Her standing, Her consoling presence. Chapters Five, Six, and Seven speak to us of the closeness, the proximity, the friendship that sustains, educates, and carries us. Chapter Eight leads us to Golgotha, to the mystery of suffering. Chapters Nine and Ten bring out the light of a new life, of a prevailing hope.

The voyage will also take you to our volunteers' deeper journey from the moment in which they recognize the compelling summons to *"Go forth from your land and from your father's house to a land that I will show you"* (Genesis 12:1) (Chapter One), to that bittersweet moment in which they must leave that very land they now call their new home, to return to their homeland, never to be the same man or woman again (Chapter Ten)!

Chapter by chapter, you will share in the voluntcers' anxieties, losses, tears, and joys. You will grab their hands and thus enter their new culture, learn a new language, and acquire a new gaze. With them, you will marvel at and struggle to enter into an intense, intentional communal life, and the life of a neighborhood, as they learn how to love and be loved. Carried by thcm, you will enter Alice's nursing home room compelled by her despairing cry; receive confession from Alex; and become a calming presence to little Net, whispering that he is a good child. Together with them, you will start to feel at home among heaps of trash, dirt soil, and barred windows. You will stand in awe at the persistence of human dignity found in a garbage dump. You will hold the hand of dying Dona Gloria, as she says, "It is done. Time to go."

Throughout the ages, every human heart has repeatedly cried out with the prophet Isaiah: *"If only you would rend the Heaven and come down!"*(Isaiah 64:1–2) Even to this very day, God continues to answer with the same method: by showing Himself through man. These pages are peopled with humble human hearts who invite you to venture on the journey to the Heart of a loving Father—a journey from which no one comes back unchanged. May you, too, be granted the grace of coming out consoled, healed, and filled with an abiding hope.

Chapter One

Quick, Open! It's God Coming to Love Us!

That Question, Deeper Than All the Others

Katie — El Salvador

"I simply argue that the cross be raised again at the center of the marketplace,
As well as on the steeple of the Church. I am recovering the claim that Jesus was not crucified
In a cathedral between two candles, but on a cross between two thieves.
On the town garbage heap.
At a crossroad, so cosmopolitan that they had to write His title in Hebrew, Latin and Greek.
At the kind of place where cynics talk smut, and thieves curse and soldiers gamble.
Because that is where He died and that is what He died about.
And that is where Church people ought to be, and what Church people should be about.

— George MacLeod,
quoted in *Streetwalking with Jesus*, by John Green

I remember when I told my parents that I was going on mission to El Salvador. I think it was worse than going to the other side of the world in Thailand. My Mom said, "You mean where Jean Donovan and Oscar Romero were murdered?"

My Dad said, "You mean one of the most dangerous countries in Central America because of gang violence, volcanoes, and natural disasters? *That* El Salvador?"

They were right about all these facts. I calmly replied, "Yes, *that* El Salvador." Before I could even think, this escaped my mouth, "Where did you think Jesus would live?" I think I was as surprised as they were to hear that! Being quite excellent parents and wonderful people, they gave me their blessing, entrusting me as they always do to God.

I have not forgotten that little question. I did not intend to be snarky or self-righteous, and indeed I had the same questions and fears. Probably because I am called to be here, it is easier for me to ask the question, deeper than all the others, of where God might be waiting for me. It is easier for me to see that here, in the poorest part of the capital of the poorest country in Central America, in this slum that others say is "godforsaken"—God has not forsaken His people.

An Enthusiastic Yes!

Grace – Argentina

I remember distinctly the first time I felt called to go on a mission with Con-solatio. My final semester of college was looming before me and I was wondering what I should do after graduation. In the silence, Con-solatio came to mind. My sister had just returned from a mission with this community, and I had witnessed through her the beauty of their missions. I reflected on this incredible possibility for a moment, but then thoughts of fundraising and being sent to a country not of my choosing began to intimidate me, and within five minutes I pushed the idea aside.

I graduated from Oakland University in April and in the following month left for Argentina to teach English for a year. Upon arriving in the enormous capital city of Buenos Aires, which is home to almost half of the country's population, I found myself feeling very alone; but then I met Con-solatio! The whole community in Buenos Aires welcomed me, a lonely and homesick Yankee (the name Argentinians use for all people from the US) and gave me a home among them. I began spending Fridays at the house in the poor neighborhood of *Villa Jardín* and attending all the community outings and events.

It was not surprising, then, when I asked to share in their mission completely and live as a volunteer in the house, that their response was an enthusiastic, "Yes!" I thank God for leading me down this unique path. It was only after experiencing loneliness and receiving the love of the Con-solatio community that I realized the importance of the mission.

No "Undo" Button

Charlie – Chile

After studying and working for years, graduating from college, and finishing two internships, I decided to do the most logical thing: leave all that I had worked for in the US. Right? Did I make the right choice? Should I have stayed and followed in line, found an apartment, bought a car, and started working? Clearly this thought crossed my mind. I thought, prayed, and talked a lot about this path before I followed it.

When I was just starting high school, I saw the movie *The Mission*, where a missionary goes deep into the jungle to work to convert an Indigenous village; through friendship, understanding, and time, the Indigenous peoples begin to accept him. After seeing this Indiana Jones style adventure for God, I was hooked; not only was this an adventure, but it was one with a purpose beyond this world. So, after all of my schooling and working, I finally made the hard decision to leave and live in a completely new country and new culture, with new people and a mission!

Just before touchdown on the morning of September 13, 2019, I got my first glimpse of Chile. I really knew very little about it. Looking out the plane window, I was presented with an incredible patchwork of flat farmland surrounded by immense and rugged mountains. As the wheels touched the ground, I experienced a flood of emotions unlike any I had felt before. There was no going back; there was no "undo" button to press. I was in Chile, over 5,000 miles away from my home. I had just made the biggest decision of my life, and I really had no idea what that meant.

Broken Concrete Streets, Wired Windows, and an Abiding Presence

Grayson – Argentina

Today is day 42 of my life in *Villa Jardín*, a *barrio* of Buenos Aires some 30 minutes outside the city center. Six weeks ago, after leaving the stifling summer heat of New York City, I landed on an overcast and blustery Argentinian winter day and was greeted at the airport by two members of the Con-solatio community, Juan and Enzo. Both of them, to my surprise, planted kisses on my cheek–the customary Argentinian greeting. After taking two bus trips from the airport, we arrived at the slum, walking through streets of uneven and broken concrete with scattered trash and the occasional droppings of the many stray cats and dogs here. We ducked into a narrow street, barely the width of our shoulders, turned into another narrow pass which opened into a wider street, and we were suddenly there, facing the Con-solatio home with its turquoise front and yellow wiring protecting the window. Our street is typical of the slum: rows of houses with no space in between, some houses with smooth concrete and finished roofs and an occasional protected window, some with uneven layers of brick and sheet metal–called *chapa*–for roofing.

Stepping inside, I was warmly greeted by three smiling faces– those of Rebeka, Nana, and Ingrid. Our home is a humble space, like the surrounding area, with a concrete floor throughout; two bedrooms and bathrooms, one for the men and one for the women; one bedroom for visitors; a chapel; a kitchen/dining area; and a patio in the back where we wash our clothes by hand and hang them to dry.

After settling in and dropping my bags off, I ventured out into the slum with Juan and Rebeka to meet some of our friends. This is perhaps my strongest first impression of the life of our community in *Villa Jardín*: in my first few days, time and time again, I saw signs of the trust, friendship, and love between us and the people of the slum. Walking in the streets or visiting our friends, I saw face after face light up upon seeing us. Many times, invitations were extended for lunch, dinner, tea, coffee, or *mate*–the traditional Argentinian drink, a bitter herb blend served in a small, gourd-like container, sipped through a *bombilla*, a metal straw that also serves as a strainer so you don't directly ingest the herbs. The kids in the neighborhood ran up to us for kisses and hugs, jumping into our arms and often asking to be spun in circles.

When I arrived in the slum, there were seven of us in the community: Juan (Jean, 21) from France, Enzo (24) from Argentina, Rebeka (20) from Germany, Ingrid (24) from Peru, Nana (32) from Colombia, and Aurélie (29) from France. Last week, we held going away parties and Masses for Juan and Enzo, both of whom have now left us. For my first month, Juan and Enzo were informally orienting me to life in the slum, teaching me the ins and outs, and giving me help and encouragement with my Spanish. I'm very grateful for their help and advice and am sorry to see them go.

Nonetheless, life goes on, and the five of us are expecting a new member in November. The changing composition of the community has been a constant reality for the entire 14 years of our presence in *Villa Jardín*, yet despite the turnover and the arrival of new members, the friendship with the community stays the same. The model is the same for all communities through-out the world: older members introduce and orient the newer members and wisdom is passed on, creating a unique dialectic of continuity and change in a friendship that remains essentially the same. The source of this friendship comes from the fact that our life is rooted in prayer. Stated simply, this is a recognition that our love for the community, our slum, is not something that we create of ourselves. For love to be given, it first has to be received. This is something that is becoming more and more concrete to me as the weeks pass.

This is where the volunteers of Con-solatio find their mission, in the middle of this drama of the human heart. We split our time between the chapel and the streets of *Villa Jardín*, communicating love and friendship as signs of the ultimate Source of love that knows and loves us thoroughly and unconditionally. Our mission is not to change the people around us, start programs, or give material aid, though those actions may certainly be charitable. Primarily, our mission is to be an abiding presence: to be with the people in their lives and to listen to them. My first six weeks here have been a tumultuous orientation to this life, whether that be speaking and listening to our friends and neighbors in my (thus far) clumsy Spanish, spending part of the day with the kids in the slum, sitting in on their Catechism classes and playing soccer with them, or visiting the elderly or the AIDS and tuberculosis patients in the nearby children's hospital.

I Have Returned to the State of a Child

Emily – Brazil

I am writing to you from Salvador de Bahia, Brazil in a place called *La Fazenda do Natal* (The Christmas Farm). Set at the edge of a forest, surrounded by nature, and where the stars shine ever so brightly at night, it is a location of peace and tranquility. It consists of about seven or eight houses and a chapel, where volunteers, permanent volunteers, children, and families live. *La Fazenda* is structured first and foremost as a place of hospitality and a place to receive people who are in difficult situations and who live with us for a time until they can get back on their feet. We have a brother and sister living here who are from a single-mother home. We take them to and from school every day and help them with their homework, and every weekend they return to their house. There are two brothers, also from a single mother, who live in the *Fazenda* because their mother struggles with drug addiction and does not feel capable of taking care of them. She comes to visit the *Fazenda* every now and then to see them. Everyone here has a history to share. We live a simple life, full of the everyday tasks of housekeeping, cooking, helping the kids with homework, and weekly visits to neighborhoods nearby.

In the *Fazenda*, I have returned to the state of a child, following the community in confidence when I do not understand everything in a culture I am discovering. Portuguese is similar to Spanish; therefore, I can understand a great deal (when the people speak slowly) and I speak a mixture of the two. Little by little, I am progressing. Brazil is a country bursting with life, with many hills and valleys, all green and luscious, and people full of joy and spirit. With the country in a rough position economically and politically, there is a large part of the population without work. We find many of our friends in difficult positions for this reason. One of my first encounters during the neighborhood visits was with a woman who within a few minutes began to recount various tragedies that occurred throughout her life. She has a son who passed away a few months ago from a gun accident, a husband who abandoned her, a lost job, and a daughter with autism to take care of. I was surprised by her vulnerability; the people here are very open and frank, I am discovering. There was nothing I could say to her, because I could speak very little, but she did not need us to say anything because there was nothing to say. She needed someone to listen; she needed to let it all out. However, despite all of her suffering, she was not in despair; she has faith and a fighting spirit to continue every day. At the end of the visit, we prayed together, the best and only thing we have to give.

I would like to introduce you to someone I will name "Rose," because that is what she is, the most beautiful rose! Rose has been living in the *Fazenda* for about 22 years. She is originally from Croatia but traveled a lot as a model. She has no family or home but the *Fazenda,* and she has schizophrenia. Amidst all of her peculiarities and visions, she has an enormous heart. Rose is my teacher, the person whom I observe to learn how to live life here. She takes care of the chapel like it is the most precious thing on earth, constantly cleaning it, lighting the candles, and joining us for all our prayers. Rose helps clean the porches of every house and the areas around the trees as well. She loves the children and cares for them with a special tenderness. It is a very simple life, but she does every task with a smile, attention, and love.

A Fascinating Language, An Enculturated Heart

Naomi – Thailand

Learning Thai is slowly coming. Four mornings a week I go to Thai school. We have four teachers who switch hours in one-on-one sessions, and the school is small with few students. Consolatio volunteers have been receiving instruction from the same teachers for more than 15 years, and it is such a blessing! Our teachers know our rhythm of life, what we do, and the purpose of our mission, and have known about or personally encountered some of our friends in our neighborhood. In class, sometimes they speak about our friends whom I have yet to meet! Through many ways I see that although these four women are teachers, our relationship with them began before I came, and it is deep and trustful, open to conversations about topics ranging from food and Thai culture to God and the human heart. Sometimes I am surprised by their honesty and depth; it is a friendship. We ride the same bus sometimes as one of our teachers, and our relationship with her outside class influences our conversations in class. This kind of student-teacher relationship is new to me; I hear about difficulties and joys in the daily life of middle-aged Thai women, politics of Thai people, what natives think about foreigners, and anything you can think of. Since every person needs the presence of God, my time at school is another opportunity for friendship.

Going to Thai school is also a way to live in solidarity with the children who also go to school. The other day Nong, a 10-year-old neighbor, passed our door as Marianne and I were leaving our house in the morning for school. I saw that he had a backpack and wore his designated school uniform, which I have seen him wear only a few times. We also had our backpacks and walking sandals.

"Good morning," I said. Nong looked sleepy, which I was, too. I was thinking about what he could have been doing the night before: messing around in the streets, coming to our house to yell our names, and running around with other neighborhood kids, not doing school work.

"How are you?" I asked.

"Fine," he said, quietly nodding his head.

"Where are you going?" Marianne asked him.

"School," he said, "Where are you going?"

"Thai school," we said. He seemed a little surprised at this. I said that he learns and that we learn also. He nodded his head, we said goodbye, and he continued on his way. Marianne and I walked in the opposite direction in our *soi* (small street) and saw other children wearing uniforms who were also going to school. For me, this morning was a time of solidarity with the children; waking up early to walk to the bus stop, to ride the same bus as the kids and the adults off to work, to leave the house to be educated. It is a beautiful gift to live like the people, like the children, like Nong.

The Thai language is fascinating, as it seems to influence Thai people's way of thinking and being. As I become enculturated, new words continue to open my mind and heart to the reality of Thais. Feelings and emotions, for example, are spoken of in relation to the heart. A person who is good has a "good heart"; when someone frightens you, your "heart falls"; when you are sad, you have a "broken heart"; when you understand the meaning of something, it "enters the heart." The Thai language is helping to light for me an image of the Thai heart so that I may see it and enter into it more deeply.

No Alarm Clock, No Upscale Supermarket, and Lots of Birthday Cakes

Julian – Philippines

In the morning, while I am still lying comfortably in my bed, I am usually awakened by the sound of the children calling our names. *"Kuuuya* Johnny . . . *Aaaate* Cecilia!" *(Kuya* means older brother and *Ate* means older sister). I honestly think that I have used my alarm clock only three or four times during my first two months here because I am usually awakened by the calling of the children before my alarm can go off. When I walk downstairs to brush my teeth, there are always kids looking through the shades of the window of our house.

We start the day with prayer at 7 a.m. in the chapel of our house. After prayer, we eat breakfast and then use our mornings to do miscellaneous tasks around the house. Some mornings we clean the house and other mornings we study the Tagalog language. We can also do our laundry; however, doing laundry here is not as simple as putting one's clothes in a machine and pressing a few buttons, since we do not have a laundry machine here. We have to do the laundry by hand and dry it by hanging it outside.

Every day one of us is assigned to cook lunch. On my day to cook, I go to the market at 11 a.m. to buy the fruits and vegetables. Since we live in the same neighborhood with the poor, we also try to eat the same food that they would eat, meaning that we buy the street food from the local market rather than go to an upscale supermarket for food. On the way to the market, I am always crowded and followed by the children who want to help with the cooking. When I get back to the house with the food, I have the unfortunate task of choosing three children out of about 10 who want to cook. Their presence makes cooking an exciting and fun experience. With the little Tagalog that I know, I try and tell the children to wash their hands and to cut the vegetables. *"Maghugas ang kamay.* Wash your hands. *Ingat ka.* Be careful."What is funny is that the children, who are about seven to eight years old, know more about how to cook than I do! After cooking lunch, we eat around noon. After lunch, we take a siesta until 2:30 p.m.

In the afternoon, one of us stays at home to welcome the children into the house and play with them, while the rest of us go out in pairs to visit our friends in different parts of the neighborhood.

After our afternoon visits, the whole community attends Mass at 6 p.m. at the local church. After Mass, we all walk home and eat dinner around 8 p.m. On some nights, we will celebrate the birthday of one of the children in our neighborhood. Believe it or not, the poor in our neighborhood usually do not celebrate their children's birthdays since they are too poor to buy a present or even buy a birthday cake for them. In our birthday celebrations, we sing "Happy Birthday" and have the child make a wish and blow out the candle. This may seem very routine to many of you, but for these children, it is something of a rarity. It is really beautiful to see the smile on the child's face as they blow out the candle and make a wish. After dinner, we recite night prayer and then have some free time before we go to bed.

Some of the Most Surreal Experiences of My Life

Kelsi — India

Just the other day, Chrisanne, Latha, and I tied our best sarees to attend the wedding of a Muslim friend. We spent nearly two hours dressing, doing hair and makeup, and picking out the proper jewelry. We headed to the bus for an hour-long ride to the venue and spent the morning with the family sharing in their joy over the happy union taking place. When we arrived home in late afternoon, we received the news that Selvi, a very dear friend, had passed away. She had been ill for some time and suffered greatly before the Lord finally called her home. After they removed Selvi's body from the house, the three of us and another friend remained to pray for her soul and her family. To sit in the place where she lived, suffered, and died, and to pray over the sound of her four grown children along with other friends and relatives as they wailed and moaned over her lifeless figure just a few feet away was probably the most intense experience of my entire mission and one of the most surreal experiences of my life. After praying the Chaplet of Divine Mercy, the Rosary, and several small prayers from the heart, we told them we would be back the next day, and we took our leave.

According to Tamil custom, one must bathe and change clothing before entering the household after a funeral or wake. We weren't able to quite manage as our bathroom is inside the house, but we were all more than happy to wash up after such an ordeal. When we were all changed and squeaky clean, we quickly marched in a torrential downpour to the house of Joyce Mary to celebrate her birthday. She was very happy to see us and informed us that the bracelets we gave her as a gift were the only things she had received. She fed us and after spending some time, we went home for good.

Sometimes, especially on days like these, I look at my life and think . . . is this even possible? Did I really just attend my first Muslim wedding, the wake of a friend, and a birthday party in the same day? And then I realize that of course it's possible! When we let the Spirit lead us, anything is possible. The really crazy part is that days like these aren't as rare as one might think. We never know what the day has in store for us when we open our eyes at 5:30 a.m. every morning. All I can say is there is rarely a dull moment for the *"Chengalpet* sisters,*"* but we try to roll with the punches and take it all as it comes. We usually aren't surprised at a day like this anymore. Now this is our life as we know it and we agree that we wouldn't have it any other way.

Continuous "Yeses" to the Painful Little Interruptions

Madeleine – Argentina

Every day of ours has a structure, a schedule of hours that we follow. The hours are something we have to work to be faithful to, and with the events that occur, the various people that come and stay with us for weekends, the friends in the neighborhood who ask us to accompany them to medical appointments or with whom we go on outings, it can be difficult to stay on task: to find the time just to clean the house, to cook, to pray, to have our weekly meetings. It can be easy to go on efficiency autopilot, to say "no" to everything that might slow one down, that might "get in the way" of one accomplishing the next thing on the agenda. *"Gringa"* that I am, I can see I'm even more hardwired in this way than the others of my community. When there is an interruption, when someone won't stop talking, when everyone walks so slow, I sometimes feel like it will actually kill me. We came here to be missionaries, to live this life we believe God called us to! We have to be obedient to our agenda, we don't have TIME for interruptions! Right? Right. Well. Let me introduce you to a "friend," a woman named Madeleine Delbrel (1904–1964). I want to share the new gaze she has taught me to have on interruptions and the will of God.

"For us, the tiny circumstances of life are faithful 'superiors.' They do not leave us alone for a moment; and the 'yeses' we have to say to them follow continuously, one after the other."– Madeleine Delbrel

"Ohhhh, no!" I thought to myself, when I heard the knock on the door. Emmanuel and I were just finishing chopping apples to make a crumble for a birthday party we were to have that night. It's 2:20, and all I want to do is sleep for 30 minutes before the Rosary. *Oyya.* Deep breath. "Oh! Margarita." She's a relatively new friend. Her cancer has come back. Sometimes her face is gray and clammy from pain and exhaustion. But—almost every time—she wants to receive us. Now, for the second time in a week, she's actually come to our house, looking for us.

Interruption. Okay. Yes!

"Pasa, Pasa! Come in." She sits down, smiling—but behind the smile, something heavy today, something weary in her face. We chop. She tells us the latest on her tests, that she's waiting still for the results. Then she'll know what to expect, what kind of outcome she can hope for. She has a passion for baking. She makes the most elaborate, beautiful cakes.

"How do we make the dough?" Emmanuel asks. I glance at him. He knows. But Margarita is delighted to show him. And the next moment she's up, standing at the counter, her hands in the dough. We're cracking jokes at Emmanuel. Her eyes spark. There's light. Ah. It's 3:00 already. The others enter, rested from their siesta to pray the Rosary. Margarita sits with us, and we pray. And the tension that was just under the surface of her face is gone. And the tension under the surface of my face—oh! It's gone.

"When we surrender to [the tiny circumstances of our life] without resistance, we find ourselves wonderfully liberated from ourselves. We float in Providence like a cork on the ocean waters."— Madeleine Delbrel

Weary. Winter. Cold. It's already dark. We enter the house after an afternoon visiting the hospital of Muniz. Maria, my fellow volunteer, is already there, so why is the house dark? *"No hay luz.* There's no electricity." Not again! There—setting the table in the cold room, in the dim light of candles—is Maria, and—oh! Ezequiel. Ezequiel is an adolescent who constantly comes around—tap, tap, tapping on our window—asking for our attention, wanting to enter, wanting to be with us. If there is anyone who stretches my patience, it is Ezequiel. When he enters and stomps around and grabs a butter knife to brandish in the air in front of our faces or turns the never quite dry (oh humid Argentina!) dish towels into a game of war or yells in our ears or snickers when we pray, it just about kills me. Oh, Maria! What faith you have in humanity. Tired, cold, hungry. Deep breath.

Interruption. Please not right now. Okay. Yes.

We enter the chapel to sing evening prayer. Maria struggles to hold her prayer book in one hand and the candle in the other as we stand to begin. Ezequiel, lanky, awkward in his oversized shoes, steps quietly to her side and—so gently—takes the candle from her hand and holds it just so. There he stands, erect, quiet, attentive to helping Maria, throughout every psalm and prayer. Not one snicker. Who is this? We sit around the dim table to eat, Ezequiel—eager in his role as our chef—jumps to his feet to serve. He fills our glasses with water. "Madeleine, ¿Quieres esto? ¿Quieres más? Madeleine, would you like this? Would you like more?" Oh. Okay, God. Yes. Yes!

"Because we find that love is work enough for us, we don't take the time to categorize what we are doing as either 'contemplation' or 'action.' We find that prayer is action and action is prayer. It seems to us that truly loving action is filled with light."— Madeleine Delbrel

It's my *permanencia*. This means it's my day to cook, to lead prayers, to be in charge of the household and receiving visitors. It can be stressful, trying to get it all done. Mid-morning, sun shining, I leave the house armed with my empty bag and grocery list. Santiago and Luna, six and eight, our little next-door neighbors, are out in the passageway, pushing each other in a plastic toy car. "Madeleeeeine!! *¿A dónde vas???* *¿Podemos ir contigo!??* Where are you going? Can we go with you?" Ohhhh. Ummm. Well. Definitely this will slow me down. But already, permission was being secured from their papa, and in the next moment I had a helper carrying my bag and one little hand in each of mine. I laugh! Okay! Yes! *¡Vamos!* We go first to the *carnicería* (butcher) to buy chicken and then to the *verdulería* (greengrocer) to choose our fruits and vegetables. After insisting on sharing half the weight of the bags on the walk home, Santiago and Luna pass the whole morning with me: chopping vegetables, helping arrange the tomatoes on top of the *pasqualina* (tart), begging to get to whisk the eggs. Haha, okay, okay, every one of us gets their turn. Then pop our creation in the oven. And the next moment, Santiago wants to dance, and sing bits of the pop songs that blast from various houses of the *barrio*.

And it took a long time to cook that morning, and we were a little late for lunch and that was okay. Yes! I think that was just fine.

"And this life becomes a celebration. Each tiny act is an extraordinary event, in which heaven is given to us, and we are able to give heaven to others. Is the doorbell ringing? Quick, open the door! It's God coming to love us. Is someone asking us to do something? Here you are! . . . it's God coming to love us. Is it time to sit down for lunch? Let's go—it's God coming to love us. Let's let Him."—Madeleine Delbrel

And so, yes, we are faithful to the hours, to our "work," to our plans, to our best guesses at what is the will of God for us on any given day. This is important. But then, maybe, quite often, our task is simply to welcome with love the encounters that march into our lives, without our asking them to—that maybe, much as we try to reach Him, God comes to us. Do we receive Him? So now—yes!—to the painful little interruptions that kill us just a little bit—because, ah! What joy!

Every Stranger Is a Life Waiting to Be Told

Armando – Chile

I sit outside our house on this beautiful Sunday evening. The smell of fresh-baked bread lingers through our neighborhood. The sun is giving its farewell before sinking into the ocean. One by one the lights from within the houses ignite to imitate the stars in the night sky. Although it is a school night, the children continue to play. The *micro* (public bus) makes its last stop in our street before heading home. Friends passing by shout goodnight, and I echo their shouts in return. The more I am here, the more that I notice these moments as gifts. Our daily lives consist of these tiny gifts that remind us that we are home. These moments are not as new as they were the first months living in *Porvenir Bajo*, our neighborhood. But they mean a lot to me because they are constant reminders of how far God has led me here. These moments are profoundly marked in my heart. I do not feel like a stranger in a foreign land; I am home.

It is like our dear Saint Joseph Marello constantly said, "Do the ordinary in extraordinary ways." God is doing just that in our daily lives. I want to share with you something so ordinary that it often contradicts itself. Our *cotidiano* (daily habit) for us here is the transportation in *la micro*, and everyone takes it on a regular basis. It is a brief intermission that lies between the important tasks of the day. It is like clockwork; you get on, you pay, you take a receipt (especially for us keeping track of our spending), and you sit down until you arrive at your destination. Not a really

38

life-changing moment, but for me there hasn't been a micro trip where I did not start a conversation with someone. To the common eye, a stranger waiting to arrive at his stop holds no treasure, but once you begin with a simple hello, you discover that each stranger has a story. Each one has a life waiting to be told. I might never see them again, but they have made themselves hard to forget.

One day I took my seat by a woman who greeted me with her warm smile. She had a very simple presence, she was dressed modestly, and her eyes were silent and hazel. Right off the bat she knew I was heading to the market to buy fruits and vegetables (the three empty bags that I carried gave me away). Her name was Isabel, and she told me that she was heading off to the bus terminal to see her mother, a mother that she had not seen in 16 years. She confessed how excited and nervous she was, and she did not know how to react upon seeing her. She had suffered greatly with her as a child, but now she has realized that her mother was falling ill and that she could not go on without forgiving her. She told me that she wasn't Catholic, and she didn't know if God even existed, but she asked me to pray for her. We were less than five minutes away from the market and 15 minutes to the terminal. I prayed with her until we arrived at her destination. I asked her if she would like me to accompany her. She smiled and stated that I already had, and she felt confident to see her mother now. She told me the number of the other *micro* to take to return to the market (she also took notice that we had passed it). She thanked me and calmly exited and entered into the crowd in the terminal.

The same day when I was returning from the market carrying the three heavy loads, a man quickly exited the *micro* to help me with my bags. This is not the first time someone generously came to my aid. Sitting down I can see an elderly man offering his seat to a mother carrying her child. I can see musicians entertaining the passengers, vendors working hard to earn money, sailors heading to their duty, and students to their studies. Each one with a destination and others with nowhere to go, who stare out the window waiting for someone to talk to. A conversation to pass the time and to break the loneliness. A precious life and a story waiting to be told. An encounter of friendship that is waiting to blossom. They are waiting for us.

Chapter Two
Our Slum Is Our Cloister

Consoling the Most Suffering of Hearts

Kelsey – Uruguay

Indeed, our day is structured around prayer, and it is what gives meaning to our every action. We sing the liturgy (morning prayer, vespers, and night prayer) together, pray the Rosary together in the afternoon with our little friends, have time for personal scriptural and spiritual reading, and attend Mass every day. Each morning, we each spend an hour alone with Christ in the chapel in Adoration—what a joy and consolation it is to have this intimate time every day with Our Lord! If our sole mission were to console the heart of Christ in the middle of this suffering slum—and indeed at moments it seems to be the only certain thing in this mysterious mission I seek to understand—it would be more than enough! However, we have also been entrusted with the incredible opportunity to encounter and embrace our neighbors, to be the Presence of Christ to our friends who suffer, to walk the streets of our *barrio* as living tabernacles.

Contemplating While Running Errands

Marian – United States

When I began this mission a little over a year ago now (how time flies!), it was hard for me to accept how busy the daily life was, especially because there was office and computer work involved. I had illusions of the Con-solatio mission of *being* as opposed to *doing*, day after day spent simply *being* with our friends and community, not accomplishing tasks, not running from one thing to the next. Soon I found that in this mission there is lots of doing! Lots of work! A demanding schedule! Many events for which we have to prepare! There is much to be done and time is of the essence!

I fought with this reality for a while, but then I came to see how much fruit it was bearing, and that everything, each detail, is done for the service of Christ in the faces and hearts of our friends. When discussing this one day on the subway with Melanie, she said, "It is not a question of being *or* doing; it is learning how to be *while* doing." Ah-ha! Wow! What a revelation that resonates so deeply in me! This place of tension is the arena of true growth. To be open to God's Presence right in the middle of my work, rather than escaping into or from work, is an exercise—and even more, a begging for grace. I have so much to learn! Laetitia, one of the other members of my community, has a little note under her computer, "God is here." What a practice to steep every moment in this constant companionship. I am not alone! The One who has sent me on this mission remains with me, leads me. He moves and lives and breathes in me, and I in Him! This changes everything.

A beautiful friend of ours, Karen, came over for lunch recently and told us, "We are most powerful when we are still and silent." This struck me. How true! Yes, we need to find those moments when we can sit in still, silent contemplation. This we are blessed to experience here every morning in our hour of Adoration; but also, I think we can carry this out into our emailing, our cooking, our errand-running, our bed-making, and our visiting with each person given to us today. This is really the whole point! That our prayer would bear fruit in the tangible world, that His Presence would become concrete in our daily gestures and work. As my dearest Mom always says, "Grace is only operative in reality."

Raw and Unveiled Before Him

Brittany – Ecuador

"The more we receive in silent prayer, the more we can give in our active life. We need silence to be able to touch souls." – St. Teresa of Calcutta

Silence.

Every month of this mission I go on a 24-hour silent retreat. The idea is that it is important in our ministry to take time, as Jesus did, to go "into the desert," to pray alone, and to listen to the Father's voice.

Previously, I thought silence was a synonym for words like dull, lifeless, and boring, but I've often heard, "God speaks in the silence of the heart." Why is that? It is because when there is silence, we can finally hear His voice. We are unmasked in silence. Busyness often serves as a veil, masking who we are when the activities cease. Silence unveils. Silence reveals.

I've learned, though, that external quiet is not necessary for living an attitude of silence before God. For instance: I live in a city of four million people, the thin walls of my neighbors' houses touch mine, ships are loading 24/7 on my street, and the rap song "Boots with the Fur 'Low'" by Flo Rida randomly started playing outside my window while I was in the adoration chapel the other day. If I can only hear Him when there is external quiet or I am at the retreat center, I'm doomed. Yet silence is not merely not hearing any noise; it is practicing quieting the heart to hear His voice.

Silence is taking time to be still and reflect. It is making time to contemplate and cherish. In silence, we become aware. In reflection, we see. Sin is found and repentance can be made. When we allow for moments to be emptied of mindless chatter and constant clamor of heart, we are left to ourselves . . . ourselves and God. We are left to think and to be raw before Him.

I no longer think of silence as dull, lifeless, or boring. Silence is an exciting invitation. It is an invitation to a deeper understanding of the life we are living and the person He created each of us to be.

The Mysterious Presence That Unites Us

Kelsey – Uruguay

In reality, we are ever blessed to have much time to pray every day (though it never seems to be enough!), and we spend half of our day in the home cleaning, cooking, and praying. We seek to live the simple life of the Holy Family in Nazareth. For two months, we've been making homemade bread (much cheaper and better tasting) every day, we have a few plants and herbs to tend, grass that grows very quickly, and there is always something to wash! These moments that seem so ordinary are those which sanctify us.

Sometimes the Lord grants us the privilege of seeing the fruits of our contemplative life, like in our friend Edith. Edith is a 74-year-old woman whom we met in *Las Crocantes*, the Crunchies, a group of elderly women friends (so named for the sound that their bones make) who get together every Friday in a parish salon to chat and share time together. They do not speak about God, and many women come who don't belong to the parish. Yet the women of the parish are truly missionaries, sharing Christ's love through their friendship, and thus inspiring some of the women to go to Mass—like Edith! After years of not believing in God, Edith came to the Mass for the first time in over a decade. The next day, we visited her in her home and listened to her full story of faith: a confession! With humility, she asked us basic questions about the Church and called her sister during the visit to find out if she was baptized. She has now started classes to receive baptism this Easter. She continues going to Mass every week and grows in her faith without turning back. We did not do anything to bring Edith back to the faith, but I wonder if our presence in a chapel three blocks from her home every day didn't influence her conversion. This mysterious Presence unites us with so many Uruguayans that say they have no faith but express their faith equally—like the thousands that united to pray a Rosary for families this January on the beach, or that went to the Grotto of Lourdes near our home for the Feast Day. I now pray that our life of prayer and the simplicity of our family life would bring peace to this area that so desperately needs it.

The Face I Seek, the Eyes I Find

Anna – Peru

Solo mírame. Solo mírame. Just look at me. These words repeated over and over in my head during this past month. Keep your eyes fixed on me. I went on mission as a *buscadora de Dios* (seeker of God). I came to Peru looking for Christ's face—and I found myself looking into the eyes of little nine-year-old Esperanza as she tried to "puppy dog face" me into giving her some chocolate, the eyes of *Abuela* Lily as she laid in her bed and contemplated the ceiling, the eyes of Jasmine as they darted back and forth at the same rate as her confused thoughts that sprang from mental illness . . . Christ became concrete.

From Her Broken Body, to His Broken One

Michael – Brazil

Every Wednesday and Thursday morning, we go to Mass
in a church at the ocean's edge. I first met Ana, walking out of
that church, around April. She was about 50, with puffy cheeks;
ragged, dirt-caked clothes; and tired eyes, and she was sitting on
a wall separating the sidewalk from the sand. As I was walking
past, I smiled at her and she responded, almost automatically, by
asking for money. Not having anything, I gave an apologetic shrug
and then sat down with her, asked her name, how long she'd lived
in Salvador, and about her family. She didn't respond very eagerly
and continued to ask for money, food, and socks throughout the
conversation. One of the challenges of living a mission based on
presence, on simply being with, is that the people whom we're
trying to engage are often crushed by so many material needs that
at times they initially don't seem all that interested in what we're
offering. They need so much that we can't give. Often it seems
they would much rather have a bowl of soup or a pair of shoes
than a friend, and while we're sometimes able to offer something
small, we generally don't have anything material to give, and
we just try to continue humbly offering our time and attention.

Yet often, with time, that hunger for a presence, for a friend,
for a space where they'll be listened to and valued—a hunger that,
after a year here, I'm seeing more and more clearly as present
in everyone, a hunger that I've found within myself and within
my community as much as out in our neighborhood—emerges

beneath those material needs. That's what happened with Ana. As the months went by, I saw her every few weeks in the same spot. One morning when I had a little money, I went with her to buy a sandwich and spent most of the morning with her, but it was generally just sitting with her for a few minutes after Mass. Some mornings she was responsive, some days closed and distant; some days ready to laugh, other days a little deflated; some days sober, some days not. Over the weeks, I started looking for her as I left the church, and little by little she became a part of my life here.

Then, last week, I was about to exit the church alone—they have Eucharistic Adoration every Wednesday after Mass, and I stayed for a few minutes to pray, while the rest of the community had either already left or were still praying—with my head abuzz with all the things I had to do that morning, so distracted that I almost walked past her. She was slouched in the second to last pew, awake but in a daze, and seeing her was like walking into a wall. Just the sight of her pulled me out of myself, out of the haze of all the plans I was making, and brought me back to the world, back to the present. I walked slowly toward her and sat down at her side. I don't remember if I offered a weak "hello," said her name softly, or just sat in silence; I just remember that a few seconds after I sat down, she collapsed into my lap. She didn't say anything for a long time, just lay there and squeezed, and when she did speak, I understood almost nothing. I just sat there, holding her as she held me, cradling her head when she cried and smiling with her. After about an hour, she looked up into my eyes and laughed. Shortly after laughing, she sat up again and we walked out of the church and into the sunlight together.

Part of what made the morning so powerful was that through-out the hour that I sat with Ana, the Eucharist was exposed up on the altar. Being able to look from her face to the face of Jesus, to feel her broken body in my lap and know that Jesus' broken body was present and real in the same room, made the link between her suffering and the suffering of Christ, the link between His presence on the altar and His presence in His poor, so much more tangible, and made the call to respond to that suffering and poverty more urgent.

If a Child Is Going to Be Imitating Me . . .

Jessica — Senegal

I'll admit that when I discerned and decided to volunteer with Con-solatio, spending my days with children was not even remotely on my mind. Instead of giving me what I thought I needed, God has given me exactly what I needed by sending me to this home in a neighborhood with so, so many children.

It had been 10 minutes since I had been in the chapel for my daily hour of Eucharistic Adoration. The morning had been unusually quiet, which I was thankful for, and I really desired to dive into a meditation I had brought with me into the chapel. I heard a loud knock at the door followed by the voices of Maimouna, BuNdaw, and Pape, three kids: siblings and longtime friends of Con-solatio. One of the volunteers explained to them in Wolof that they could enter into the house under the condition that they pray (a technique many children use daily to get into our house). Sighing, I began to accept that the little spiritual exercise I had hoped to accomplish was soon to be futile.

Maimouna, the older sister of the family, who is physically handicapped due to epilepsy, entered first. She has a smile that lights up her entire face, a smile in which so much life can be seen. Her heart, so in need of being accepted and loved, is so present in her smile. It's a smile that sometimes frustrates me, that I often find hard to love because it contains a lot of mischief, displayed in all the ways she misbehaves in our house. She came in and sat right next to me, and heavily stared at me while smiling, trying

54

to make me laugh as I obviously was trying so hard to keep my focus on the monstrance. I sighed and handed her a book, which isn't always good for silence because the kids start to discuss who are in the pictures.

"Who's that?"

"That's Moses."

After 15 minutes or so of that, Maimouna started to ask me, "You're finished?"

I replied, "No, a little more," not mentioning that there was 30 minutes left. Not wanting her to be encouraged to keep talking to me, I changed positions only to notice that she was imitating my every move. Noting that I had noticed her, she turned her head and gave me a big smile that melted my heart and made me laugh out loud at the same time. I hid my head again and thanked God for teaching me what it means to pray simply or "poorly." How to live the simplicity of just being there together with Him and with Maimouna, not in trying to evoke some sort of mysticism, but in just being simple, poor, and like a child. I mean, if a child is going to be imitating me, I had better be simple and like a child.

Can You Tell God What I Want to Say?

Christina – Romania

Alice is pulling my hand. I reluctantly walked with her onto this hill of old cement as she claimed to have something very important to say. I asked her why we couldn't just stay with the other kids, why we had to climb up high. Alice said, "Christina, we need to be up high, we are going to talk to God and need to get close to Him. Can you tell Him what I want to say?"

"Okay, Alice, but why don't you want to tell Him?" I asked.

"Well Christina, if Jesus were here, I think He would want to be your friend because you are very fun and good at listening. So, I think if you say my prayer to Him, He will hear you because your voice is very important." In that moment, Alice's voice was the most important one I had ever heard.

"Alice, your voice is so, so important to Jesus. When you talk to Him, everything else is quiet and He can hear you."

"Okay, Christina, I'm going to pray to our Father." I thought Alice wanted to pray an Our Father together, but when I started, "No Christina, I don't know the Our Father. I just want to talk to our Father, you know, up there?" She said this as she pointed up at the cloudy sky. So, Alice talked to God and asked Him to make her family healthier and for more snow, and I stood dumbfounded listening to this little eight-year-old. Just like that, I found His Presence on an ugly day in the form of a difficult little girl.

I Am Here So He Can Dwell

Grace – Argentina

Although he has lived right across the street from our home since its founding 21 years ago, it has only been a little over a year that Angelo began getting to know the volunteers and coming to the house. He told us on several occasions that he does not believe in God, because he asked God for things on multiple occasions and, as far as he can see, God never responded.

Once a month, our house has a night of Adoration when each member of the house takes an hour to adore the Blessed Sacrament, and we invite our neighbors to come pray with us. In June, another volunteer in my community, Pablo, invited Angelo to come pray with him during his hour and, much to my surprise, he came. One Friday in July, I saw Angelo outside his house and went to greet him. I made a joke asking if he had forgotten to shave since he is usually clean-shaven, but he appeared as if he hadn't shaved all week. "When is the prayer night, tonight or tomorrow?" he asked me. His question caught me off guard as it seemingly had nothing to do with what I had asked.

"Tomorrow," I replied.

"Okay, I'll shave tomorrow," he responded.

Sure enough, that Saturday when I entered in the chapel for my hour, Angelo was seated and clean shaven in one of the chairs, and Pablo in the other as they sat quietly before Jesus. Upon entering and seeing the three of them, I paused so as to capture the scene; it is something I never want to forget. In that moment, my mission made so much sense to me. I am here so that Jesus can dwell in this chapel and be with those whom He loves. Our Lord had been here waiting for 21 years for this moment with Angelo, with His son. If my mission had ended that night, I would have gone home happy. Jesus had the chance to be with His child.

Chapter Three

Woven Together

Not the Feel Good, Butterflies in My Stomach, Easy Love

Brittany – Ecuador

One aspect of the mission that I have been hesitant to write to you about is community life. Why have I been hesitant? Because it has been the most unexpected challenge of this mission. I've lived in community before. I get along with people alright. So, I was thinking living in community would be no big deal, nothing too new for me. Well, I stand corrected.

We are a community of members from all over the world. We all came to Ecuador with our unspoken cultural ideals, preferences, and values. Spanish, for most of us, is a weak second language. We are a range of different ages and personalities. We eat together, pray together, serve together, and make decisions together. This is unlike any community life I have experienced before. However, despite all our differences, we have one thing in common—one thing that unites us all. We were all called to this mission.

In this mission, my community has shown me the sacrificial kind of love. Carolina stayed with me all four nights I was in the hospital. I tried out dengue fever while in Ecuador. Julia washed my clothes when I was tired. Philippine gave me the last helping of food when we were both still hungry after dinner.

After five months, I can finally see through the murkiness of difficulties clouding my vision to the irreplaceable value of living in community. It has been for me a lesson in love: not the feel good, butterflies in my stomach, easy love, but the hard, when there is offense, when you don't agree kind of love. It has been a call within a call. It is a call to truly seek to love rather than to be loved. And to fail. But to try again. It has been humbling but necessary. Necessary in my faith life and necessary for living this mission well.

John 4:20 has repeatedly come to my mind, *"Whoever does not love the brother whom he can see cannot love God whom he has not seen."*

The Gift of a Loving Family

Elizabeth — Brazil

We have been contemplating a lot what it means for our mission that our Brazilian house is named after the Holy Family in a neighborhood where complicated family situations are abundant. Many girls become moms here before they are really women, and it is rare to encounter kids who grow up in a home with both of the parents who created them, and even less with parents who are married.

One day, this reality was made plain to me when I was playing with Bea and Giovanna, two sisters, in the street near their house. When she saw a man on a motorcycle turning the corner, Bea, the younger sister, ran to greet him yelling, "Daddy! Daddy!"

I turned to Giovanna who continued to play and said, "Look, your dad is arriving!"

She looked at me and said, "He's not my dad."

I thought for a moment that I had confused which of the kids are siblings and asked her, "But you and Bea are sisters, right?"

Giovanna told me, "Yeah, but each has her own Dad."

I was caught off guard by this assumption I had made, that just because the little girls are sisters they have the same dad. That's not the reality for Bea and Giovanna, and their situation is very typical of the kids in our neighborhood. These girls awoke in me a more conscious sensitivity and awareness of the dynamic of families here. More importantly, they reminded me that to make assumptions about a person or situation is to fail to see the mystery before me and to deny a person the gift that it is to share who you are with another.

As for the meaning of our house's patron, the Holy Family, we believe that the presence of our community in this neighborhood is meant to be that of a loving family. The life of a Con-solatio volunteer has three core values: prayer life, community life, and an apostolate of compassion. Each impacts and fortifies the others. So, for each of our friends to encounter a loving family in our home, we need to strive for unity among all of us in our house, just as much (if not more sometimes!) as we are striving to be present to our friends in the neighborhood. I'm sure many of you can testify to the fact that love for others starts in the home with the people you're living with, and the fact that it's easier said than done many times!

Not Just Those Whom I Choose

Natalie – Thailand

Though places like the IDC (Immigration Detention Center) are teaching me much about compassion, I'm learning that the primary place to learn true compassion is in the community, where there is nothing romantic—just human and real. Jesus' measure of love is not that which we do for those who love us, nor that which gives us pleasing results. His call to love is much higher than that. I'm learning that, for me, this call is to bring all of my relationships into tension, so that each is a living out of compassion—not just those which I choose. For instance, if it is easy for me to forgive the unkind words of an IDC prisoner, but I can't forgive the unkind words of my fellow volunteers, what do I know about Christ-like forgiveness? If I am able to listen to the ramblings of an IDC prisoner every week, but zone out or become uncharitable when my community member tells the same story again, what do I know about Christ-like patience? If I seek to understand the poor behavior of an IDC prisoner because "he has had a hard life," but am unwilling to do the same for my other community members, what do I know about Christ-like compassion? There's a long way to go, but luckily as I beg Jesus to make me more like Him, He gives me many opportunities to practice and covers all my short attempts to do His will with abundant mercy.

So I Do Not Sound Like Tarzan!

Madeleine – Argentina

Con-solatio is a kindergarten of love, an experience through which young adults can better learn what it means to truly love. Before leaving on my mission, I was not particularly interested in going to any kindergarten. Yet here I am, and I have to tell you this is so. The first lesson was quite painful for me, because I have had to accept being like a child in order to learn it. What was this "lesson"? That of accepting my need for others, my lack of self-sufficiency. This is where my mission has begun—in learning how to receive the love and generosity of my community members and even the very people I came to serve.

The primary place in which I have come to learn to receive has been in my community, from the five people with whom I share this mission: from Sixtine guiding my singing with her voice as we pray the Divine Office; from Francisco accompanying me to buy food; from Emanuel teaching me possessive pronouns so I "do not sound like Tarzan" (his words); from Gabriel and Marie giving me the words of encouragement and insight into the meaning of our life here that I need to hear. I have learned much about how to love from the way each of them has seen my poverty and responded with compassion. To receive their love with a peaceful heart I've had to accept being like a child, letting them see what I need, and accepting their generosity.

Among our friends in the neighborhood, whom I have little by little come to know, I have found other "teachers" about how

66

to live my new life and what it means to love. Luna is only 13, but after an attempt at conversing with me in which I awkwardly floundered, she taught me a handshake (no need for words there) and offered to come by the house the next day at noon to study with me and teach me Spanish. Faithful to her word, she came by at the appointed time to study with me. One Sunday after Mass, Milena, a woman who has been friends with the Con-solatio volunteers throughout the years since it began in *Villa Jardín* 26 years ago, asked if she could walk me home as we were leaving. She more or less took my hand and brought me with her to buy meat and then to a pastry shop, making me pick out a pastry for myself—then I really felt like a child! All the while she asked me questions about myself, patiently listening to my answers. Both she and Luna saw me, accepted my limitations, and took the time and attention to meet me there—to listen to me and be present with me and show me my value. Both taught me in these experiences what it is to be a Con-solatio volunteer—really, what it is to be human and merciful—and I was the one who received!

Maybe We Are Not All That Different

Anna — Peru

I always know that Roxana is at our door by her laugh. Roxana is both deaf and mute, but she has her own language which I am slowly uncovering. Sometimes she will whisper in my ear or close the door when she doesn't want anyone to hear what she is "saying." Sometimes I feel impatient with her constant presence and walk to the door with a bit of dread when I hear her laugh, but I am slowly learning that Roxana has a lot to teach me and that maybe our situations aren't all that different . . .

My first month here, I felt overwhelmed by all of the new names, culture, language, community, and rhythm of life. I wanted someone who knew me. Although having a strong foundation in Spanish has been an incredible blessing, I still often felt at a loss for being able to express myself. When I think of Roxana, I can't even begin to imagine the world she lives in: a world of silence, with few people who have the time or the patience to listen to her "talk," trapped within herself. Yet she lives with a laugh and love for us. She is extremely attentive to her environment and the needs of those around her.

In my loneliness, I realized that Jesus is always with me and knows me better than anyone could. And He loves me. Each day is an opportunity to rest in this unconditional love and allow God's love to flow through me and engulf our friends. This love inspires me to want to see Roxana; to love her in a way that is outside of words and not dependent on anything she does, but simply for her existence. It also challenges me to receive God's love through Roxana, to accept her hugs and help as a concrete experience of God's love for me.

The Beauty of Rough Edges

Mara — Ecuador

Community life isn't easy. Living with and sharing a life with other people is almost never easy, and less so when they're people you didn't pick out, with different cultures and backgrounds. On top of culture and personality differences, everybody has their own rough edges, and they usually don't fit together perfectly with the rough edges of the next person. It's precisely those rough edges that make community life something beautiful. At the end of the day, we all kneel down together in the chapel and we ask forgiveness from those we've hurt during the day and the times we affected the community by our mistakes, and we give thanks to those who gave their time, their effort, their love: thanks to David who gave up his much-needed siesta to help the neighbor with his homework, thanks to Leti who stayed up late to clean the kitchen, to Kari who saw I was having a bad day and asked me about it, to Jack for washing the plates (again), to Leo for spending time with the kids when I didn't have the patience. Above all, we give thanks to the Divine Planner, who knew exactly what He was doing when He placed us all together under the same roof. We might get on each other's nerves sometimes, but it's in choosing to love when it's most difficult to do so that we truly learn to love in its truest sense.

Living in community has shaped me, helped me, and challenged me. It has given my life structure and security amidst the often-incomprehensible mysteries of love and suffering that

I have been presented with day in and day out here; my community members have provided me with the security and the strength I need to live our mission each day through their love, encouragement, and examples. At the end of each day, I can only be grateful—often ruefully—for my community and for sharing this mission with them. It's true what they say: the best things are never easy.

Broken and Shared

Andrea – India

As often as we in the West talk about the weather, the people here in our corner of India talk about food. "How are you?" is replaced with *"Saptingelaa?* Did you eat?" from which flows an entire conversation about what, when, and how much we ate. Beyond surface-level pleasantries, I've come to treasure how food is such a beautiful way for us to share life with the Indian people. Preparing and consuming meals in our community are deeply human activities of daily life that connect us to our neighbors who greet us from their front steps as we walk by. It is a shared experience that reaches to something within us that flows from our desires to be satisfied, our capacity to receive and create, and is ultimately oriented toward our nourishment and flourishing.

Our neighbor across the street, *Suriyamma ("amma"* means mother), sees us many times a day and faithfully asks us if we've eaten every single time. The bulk of my conversations with her have been about food, and she is quick to offer tea, *idli*, or *dosa* if I ever show the slightest hint of hunger. One day, after she gave me some tea, she said, "I lost my husband on a Sunday, and so every Sunday is very difficult for me. There is a lot of tension in my mind. But when you're here, I feel free." Somehow, the trust we've built through showing our care for one another through talking about food while sitting on her front steps opened the door to sharing life in a way I wasn't expecting.

The words "Give us this day our daily bread" have taken on a new meaning for me; receiving God's Providence has become a tangible, communal experience. *Suriyamma* has shown me that not only is the food we eat broken and shared, but our lives are broken and shared. From this shared life bloom child-like trust and freedom in knowing that we're never alone. Rootedness in communion with our neighbors has allowed me to trust more deeply in the Word Incarnate, Jesus as the Bread of Life, which we receive every morning at Mass and in every moment through the faces of our friends.

Chapter Four

Love That Persists

The Unseen

Cleopatra – Philippines

You roam the streets and lie on the sidewalks
You walk among us, yet do not seem as us, to us
Someday, somewhere, you were born to someone
Somewhere, you were nursed and looked after
Someone cared for you, unseen being
Who were you once before?
Who knew you once before?
Who lost you or drove you away, once before?

Many times, I've walked or driven by without paying attention
On my merry busy way to wherever I am going
When my eyes catch your eyes, I see you
You are seen
You are someone
You are a soul
You are a person
You are a story
You are a present
You are

Your bruised body and drug-affected face hurt me
My heart aches for all the abuse and trauma you have undergone
in your life.
My heart aches for you thinking this is your only safety or option

I ask myself, does your heart still ache?
Has it stopped feeling, yearning for that which it was created for
Love?
Do you see love in my eyes?
Do you know I hurt for you?
Do you know I wish you more than this?

In this moment we share, all I can do is be present
Hear you
Be there
Listen
And Hope

As you speak, you become more and more like me
You have now moved from unseen to seen
You matter
You are here
You are beautiful and I am thankful for your existence!

Don't Leave Me Alone!

Lindsay – El Salvador

Every week our community has what we call an "i-school." Together we read a text and then use it to talk about the experiences we had during the week. We just finished reading one entitled *"El Rostro"* or *"The Face."* I was very struck by this text, particularly by the words, "the face is the visibility of the heart." I see many faces and hearts every day: the faces of children peering through our window asking to play, the face of a friend laughing and joking with us in the street, the face of a child peering into mine as they run up to hug me in the street. But the face I see the most often is one that says, *"No me dejes morir solo.* Don't leave me to die alone. Don't abandon me.*"*

I read it in the face of Maria, a 15-year-old girl, whose mother abandoned her together with her two sisters when she was only six. In her face, which tries to appear tough and indifferent, but whose eyes are often filled with tears, I read, "Please, don't leave me alone. Don't abandon me."

I see it in the face of Don Carlos, an 87-year-old man, whom we bring to the doctor and whose medications we help monitor. He is a very happy man who loves to work outside, building boxes and other odds and ends. He has three children, but they never visit him. He tells us, "I am so thankful for Con-solatio because they are the only ones who care about me." In our friendship with him, I hear the plea, *"No me dejes morir solo.* Don't leave me to die alone. Don't abandon me.*"*

When visiting some of our friends I hear, "You haven't visited in a while," or upon leaving, "I'm waiting for the next time I will see you." In this, I hear the cry, "Don't forget about me. I don't want to be alone."

In the teenagers who turn to drugs, I hear the cry, "My life is so difficult. I want something different. I want to feel something different. Don't leave me to die alone, please help me."

Isn't this the cry of all of our hearts? I know that in my own poverty of being unable to fully speak/express myself, of not understanding Spanish at the beginning, not understanding the culture or all of the problems that my friends face, this is the cry of my heart, too: "Don't leave me alone. Will you accept me in my poverty?" This is the question we all ask, and Christ answers, "Yes." My mission here is quite simple, but also challenging. It is to say with Christ, "I accept you as you are—with all of your problems, with all of your strengths and joys. I am here. I will not abandon you." I think that the simple fact that our house has been here for 21 years (and hopefully through the grace of God will be here for many more) says that we are here. We are here in the neighborhood where no one else wants to go. We are not going anywhere. We are present. Christ is here.

Where Is God?

Francesca – Romania

The church looms over the trees of the small park like a giant frosted cake. The windows are dark, and God appears to be sleeping, as if He forgot to wake up after the war. The apartment blocks surround the church; tall, gray soldiers standing at attention. Snow falls gently on their balconies, as if God is trying to make something beautiful out of something that is not. Old gypsy men scatter themselves on the streets, exposing their diseased legs, red with frostbite, hoping someone will take pity and leave a few cents.

They say with time wounds heal, but what did they ever say about scars? Scars are deceiving. They don't reveal the depths of the injuries that formed them, the intensity of the pain, the incredibility of the story. I remember a visit with a widow who lives alone. In a moment, she started crying as she remembered the Christmases of her youth, when sometimes all they had for dinner were bones in boiled water.

Yes, there is material poverty here, slums built in the hills of trash and mud, but that is not what pierces the heart. The real poverty is the lack of a sense of belonging, of identity, of humanity. The woman whose father refuses to acknowledge her existence even after 30 some years. The eight-year-old boy forced to declare before the state that neither his mom, his dad, nor the Catholic children's home wants anything to do with him. The man abandoned by his wife and kids because the only job he could find to support them took him too far from home. One of the other members of my community who lost her dad, a close friend, and her uncle all in the same year. I'm left sitting on the frozen gray sidewalk staring up at the frozen gray sky, wondering, "Where is God?"

I studied God in school, I felt Him in family and friends back home, in the simple joys of everyday life, but here, I learned that God is in the very places where I question His existence the most. He is the love of the 23-year-old young man who dedicated his life to raising Micutul and his brothers at the children's home. He is the love of Alex's 17-year-old sister who takes care of him along with her two-year-old son. He is the love I have for Elena, as rude and difficult as she might be. God is love. Life here is a shade of gray that I had never lived before, one that comes with fears and doubts I had never known. But one thing I know for sure: God is here. For all of my schooling, I have no theological explanation. I haven't witnessed any miraculous healings or families reunited. No "wow stories" without practical explanations. I have only stories of love that persists, through life, through death, and through broken families. Stories of love that can be explained only by the existence of a God.

Yeah, Yeah, the Hospital . . .
But I Need a Chat All the More!

Gabriel — Argentina

Jorge arrived at our door one day in really poor condition and asked if he could come in and talk. We happily invited him in and sat down at the table, and he proceeded to tell us part of his life story. He had much trouble drinking, breathing, and walking, and he was clearly in a lot of pain. He told us that he was in an accident two years ago where he fell three stories off a building and that he has been suffering with his health ever since. He did not know us, and we did not know him, but he said that the people in our neighborhood have great trust in Con-solatio and pointed us out to him, since he was in need of assistance. After chatting for a while, we decided that we would go to the hospital with him in order to diagnose and begin fixing his health issues.

Wednesday night, Victor and I went to his "house" to remind him of the appointment and were both very touched by the experience. He lived in a tiny, filthy, little concrete room without even a door. His few belongings were piled on the floor, covered in cockroaches and mosquitos. Jorge invited us into his room, and we began to talk. He told us that his life is very difficult because he has no money, no work, and many health problems. But right after that, he said that all of that is nothing compared to the hardest part of his life—he is alone. Living without friends or family is much harder for him than any poverty.

He told us that he did not want to go to the hospital the following morning and would rather spend time with us drinking *mate*. Victor and I tried to push the necessity of the hospital as well, but he insisted that he just wanted to talk. It is really hard to understand and fathom a loneliness like this. He is only 46 years old and literally has nobody in his life. I was very moved by Jorge's humility to recognize the necessity of a friend, as well as the courage to simply ask two much younger men. Victor and I walked back to our house in silence. That night I learned a little bit more about the mystery of suffering from our new friend, Jorge.

I Also Lost My Teeth

Mollie – Romania

Elena is a little girl from our street. A couple of weeks ago, Philippine noticed that she had an open cut on her finger and a small piece of something stuck in it, which was causing an infection. Elena needed to be brought to the emergency room as soon as possible. Her grandma refused to take her to the hospital, but she did agree to let us take her. When we got there, I realized how little basic information we had about her, or she had about herself. She doesn't have any form of identification. She couldn't answer the question of her date of birth or family name. I'd never seen this presumably confident little girl so unsure as when she was asked questions about who she was and to whom she belonged to.

When Elena was on the medical table, she squeezed my hand and looked into my eyes. I felt her discomfort as they removed the small piece of wire, but I also saw in her a pain that was buried much deeper than the metal in her finger. I was given a quick glimpse for the first time of a cry and thirst that I hadn't seen before. Once, as she explained that her dad and siblings are in another country, she stated casually: "They didn't want me, so they left me here." Another day, while we were at St. Anthony's for Mass, I explained that you can ask St. Anthony to help you find something that you've lost. She replied by saying, "Okay, I'll pray. Because I lost my dad." Then she lightened the mood like she always manages to do with, "I also lost my teeth," showing off her naked top gums.

Like many of my friendships here, my friendship with Elena is a mystery to me. In her thirsting and searching, which is only just beginning, I can only be next to her. I can only offer her a hand to squeeze and borrowed love, then entrust the rest to God.

Would He Like a Visitor?

Natalie – Thailand

One day I found Jaij (Grandmother) Bat crying in her doorway. She explained, "Abel had to go to the hospital in the middle of the night." She motioned to the corner of the room where her son, who is severely disabled, was usually lying. Indeed, the blue blanket which normally covered his motionless little body was now neatly folded and pushed up against the wall. Abel. So that was his name. Jaij shared that it would be difficult for her to go see him because getting there and back is expensive, and her now-handicapped leg prevents her from being out and about for very long. I was moved to ask, "Would he like a visitor?" As soon as the words came out of my mouth, I realized how foolish they must sound. Here I had never even spoken to him—I had just learned his name the minute before! Speaking of speaking, I wasn't even all that confident in my Thai at that point. What would I say to him? Could *he* speak?? Would he be weirded out by this random girl coming to visit him? Would Jaij? Plus, I realized, I had never even seen his face yet! How would I recognize him?? This was silly, wasn't it? Apparently not to Jaij, whose face lit up as she immediately began writing his name, the hospital, and his room on a scrap of paper for me. "Could you go see him tomorrow?"

"Of course," I answered, still unsure of what it would be like, but somehow certain that I was answering both to her and to God.

Over the next month, Thuy, Marie, and I rotated visiting Abel almost daily both in the hospital and at his house. His health would improve only to rapidly plummet even worse within a couple days. At first, I was very timid and afraid. How close was it safe to get to his face as I strained to listen to him, while he alternated between semi-coherently rambling to me and coughing up blood? As my friendship with him grew, I found myself less and less afraid. I found the courage to help feed this new friend, help him roll over, lay my hands on him as I prayed for him, to advocate for him when he needed to be changed or when water from the ceiling was leaking on him and no one had noticed. I began to really look forward to visits with him and he always begged us not to leave, asking, "When are you coming back?"

Please, May I Have a Cup of Water?

Jessica – Senegal

"Jessica, I'm thirsty! Give me a cup of water!" demanded seven-year-old Genevieve while hugging my side after evening Mass at our house, after which we tell all of the children, "See you later!" so that they can be with their families for the evening, and for us to eat dinner and finish the day.

"Genevieve! It is 'Jessica, PLEASE, may I have a cup of water?' We have to be polite," I replied, slightly frustrated because I was tired after having been with the children most of the day, and I still had a lot of other things to finish after they all left.

"Okay, okay, Jessica . . . Please may I have a cup of water?"

"Yes, Genevieve . . . you may," I said as I handed her the small blue plastic cup and rubbed her head a little, still frustrated.

She stayed attached to my side as she held the little cup to her lips with her eyes fixed upon me. The others in the community were reminding the children it was time to leave, scrambling after them. After a bit, Genevieve sighed a happy sigh, placed the cup on the counter, smiled at me with her whole face and said, "*Merci*, Jessica!" and made her way to the door.

"Okay Genevieve, it's nothing. See you tomorrow," I replied as I started to clean up in the kitchen. I reached for the cup Genevieve had just drunk from and noticed that the cup was still full of water. Annoyed at what seemed to have been a pointless five-minute exchange, I drank the water myself and went on with the other tasks of the evening.

Later that night as I was lying in my bed unable to sleep, I started to pray, holding my rosary, and started thinking about all of the things that had happened in the day, asking Mary to shed light upon them. After some time, I began to recall the encounter with Genevieve in the kitchen. The first thing I remembered was the full cup of water, but as I prayed more, I started to remember the gaze in her full eyes and the way her body was totally embracing my side. I remembered the smile she gave me as she thanked me and started to walk away . . . and then I sat up in my bed, my tired eyes widened. It hit me; when Genevieve thanked me, she wasn't thanking me for water. She was thanking me for being with her, for my presence. My eyes filled with tears, as I really started to understand. I began to understand why I am here; I began to understand what this mission is all about, what life is about. I felt so selfish for my earlier frustration, but even more than that, humbled at realizing how easily the memory of what had seemed to be this meaningless encounter, an exchange so normal in our house, could have slipped away from me. It is so easy to get caught up in doing things that we forget the real purpose: to be. To be present. I could give water like an assembly line to every child in Grand-Yoff Arafat, but most of those children would leave still thirsty. It's not about giving away water; it's about giving away my heart.

May They Grow Up to Forget My Name

Christine – Romania

There are three little boys in Mintia (the gypsy colony that we visit) that have become especially close to my heart. After only one day of playing together early-on in my mission, we developed a particular fondness for each other and since then, they have come to occupy a space so deep in my heart that I would have thought could only be reserved for my own future children. It's been eight months of countless piggyback rides, giggles, and hugs, but even after all that we've done together, last week one of the boys, Sibi, asked me, *"Cum te chema?* What's your name?"* Instead of being offended that this little boy (whom I already know I will never forget) didn't know my name yet after eight months of friendship, I just laughed. I saw it as a little reminder from God that this mission isn't about me. Sibi is not searching for *me*, for *my* companionship, for *my* love. He is looking for Christ—for *His* companionship, *His* love.

As I became aware once again that I am here in Romania to bring Christ to others, I felt liberated. If I am here to bring Christ to this little boy, what did it matter if he has already forgotten my name? If I am here trying to be Christ for others, what does it matter if I make nearly inedible food for lunch when I experiment with the things in our fridge? What does it matter if I sometimes mix up the words *picat* (fell) and *plecat* (left) when I speak in Romanian? When we consciously live for Christ, we can feel free to be ourselves, faults and all, because Christ lives in us.

While flipping through my journal recently, I came across a passage I had written at the beginning of my mission during a time when I was feeling completely useless, because I couldn't communicate with anyone. I had written, "I don't feel like the people here really need me. I know they need someone, but maybe it's not me." Now I see how I had been equally right and wrong in writing that. I was right in saying that the people here don't need me, because the One they need is Christ. Yet at the same time, they do need me, because I can bring Christ to them. They need me, but only because I am an instrument, trying to bring Christ wherever God leads me.

It makes me take my mission here much more seriously when I'm conscious of the fact that God called me here specifically to bring Christ to Sibi and my little friends in Mintia. They may grow up to forget my name or forget me altogether, but I pray that they grow up to have a special relationship with the One who called me here to love them.

A Lost Lamb!

Marian – United States

Martha is my Babushka, my sweet Russian grandmother, who lights up my days! From the first moment we met, we clicked. I just fell in love with her soft-skinned, scarf-head-wrapped self. Every Wednesday, we go to visit her only a block away from our home. It is so nice to know she's so nearby. Martha has such a comforting presence. She is a nurturing mama, salt-of-the-earth, hard-working Russian woman. She often says to me in her thick Russian accent, "I have so many babies! So many babies!"

You never know just how you'll find her, as she dwells in a cloud of dementia, usually speaking in repetitive loops, sometimes sad or delighted, quiet or chatty. I usually find her lying on her bed, resting peacefully. I sit beside her and her eyes light up. "My baby!" she exclaims with a big, big hug and kiss. She clasps her hands and delights in our visit.

This day, Martha looked different. She was resting, but her brow was furrowed, pained by a nightmare or sadness. I sat beside her, noticing that her eyes were red and puffy. As she awoke from her inner world and came into Nati's and my glance, she began to cry.

"I been crying all the day, like big baby! Only crying. I just lie here all day. No work. No walk. No one. Just lie here. I like a lost lamb in the woods. A lost lamb. No home." She cried and then began laughing. A big smile bubbling over through her tears. She looked at me, "But you! You remember me! You come to find me here! You no forget me! You thinkin' of me." She is overcome with love and pulls my head to her chest, then brings my forehead to her lips and gives me a kiss. She clasps her hands together, eyes twinkling with joy and delight, "I growing now. I growing! Someone so sweet like you, someone so beautiful!" She brings me in for a big squeeze.

Nati and I give her ashes, to which she is totally oblivious. We try to tell her, "Martha, you have ashes now for Ash Wednesday."

Not aware of what we're saying, she responds, "That's okay." This makes us laugh. She joins in our laughter, which only makes us laugh harder. She exclaims, "I crying all day and you bring me laughter! Ohhh!" We are all laughing together, heads thrown back with abandon. We say goodbye and she tells us, "Take it easy, okay?" We laugh more, and step out. I hear her say, "Oh, God! Thank Heaven they be coming to see me today!" Oh God! Thank Heaven for Martha!

Chapter Five

He Comes to Sit
in Our Trash Heaps

Dirty Eucharistic Hands

Cleopatra – Philippines

Lord, I've approached you so many times
With the hands I found and assumed were clean.
To touch your heavenly body, what an honor I am given,
So, I tried to have the cleanest hands possible.
Now Lord, I approach you with dirty Eucharistic hands!

But they are cleaner than ever before
Now I walk the streets and see your suffering body!
I see your sorrowful face
And it cries out to me to touch it and share your pain,
Your suffering, your joy!
I walk your streets and see your little ones,
Little ones who are physically dirty but full of your life.
As I hold them, hug them, kiss them, I am both filled
With their dirtiness, and most importantly
Your love!

Thank you little Ray, Bambie, Lady, Venice, and Princess.
Thank you for playing with me
For jumping on me
Thank you for yearning for God's embrace!
Thank you for showing me Christ's brokenness
Thank you for preparing me!

So, as I wait in line to receive your heavenly feast, Lord
I offer up all these whom my hands have touched this day
My hands, your instruments to love and comfort.
I offer you the Abigails, Ninets, Tricias, Carlos, Mary Maes,
Gabriels,
Rents, Vanessas, Vilmas, Jonathons, *Ate* Marissas, *Ate* Malous,
Ate Susanas, *Ate* Alohas, *Kuya* Roels, *Kuya* Renatos,
And *Ate* Josies of the world
I bring them and present them before you
As an offering!

Please take my dirty Eucharistic hands
And place your beautiful body on them
Which I will consume to be consumed myself!
I thank you my God for my dirty Eucharistic hands
May they always remain ready to be dirty and used for love!

The Unity I've Been Looking For

Justine – Senegal

"Tanga na trop!" is one of the first things I learned to say in Wolof, "It's too hot!" I hear other people saying it too, as they pile—quite literally—into buses. During Mass, the church is so packed that we sit shoulder to shoulder. I can feel the sweat dripping down my back and front. It was during Sunday Mass at St. Paul's that I realized that this discomfort, this suffering, this incarnation, is precisely what we are gathered to celebrate! My faith is not in a God distant and ethereal but in a God who became man. The physical reality is a manifestation of that incarnation: the hard-wooden pews, the smell of incense and the smell of people, sand sticking to my knees when I kneel, the choir swaying and clapping, the Eucharist at the center of it all, Christ becoming flesh.

Life here is certainly incarnate, not just in church, but everywhere. It is the body in all its wounds and scabs, in all its batik dresses and styled hair, in all the boisterous joy of the tam-tam drum. This constant sweating, uncomfortable as it is, has given me a new way of looking at life. I am sometimes troubled by the fact that life can so easily be separated into a dozen little boxes: intellectual interests, spiritual life, work, friends. Where is the unity? How can I be a whole not just a sum of parts? The shared suffering of being almost unbearably hot has made me realize that a box into which everything of life belongs is the incarnation, "in the flesh." I experience the reality of my life through my body—I

cannot separate my thoughts or even my prayers from my body!
It sounds simple; but there is the unity I've been looking for!

A Brazilian Among Brazilians

Erica – Brazil

Three days a week I take Helena to school. We spend an hour on the bus each morning smashed like sardines in standing room only. I work in a building falling apart with unruly children, we return in the dreadful afternoon heat on the bus for an hour and a half, and I come home to a wild child and a house to keep that attracts massive amounts of dirt and bugs. I may not have managed to darken my skin, change my eye color, or color my hair, but I have become one with the people I came to serve. I live the exhaustion and I walk the dirty streets. I never imagined my mission as it is. Before I left a year ago, I pictured myself as Angelina Jolie with children running behind me in the dirt streets. I pictured myself visiting many houses with little old ladies who were alone and bringing a light to the room. Instead, I have been given something greater—an understanding, a deep and true compassion for these people who have to fight to live in dignity and hope. Instead, I have been given a little boy that I can't send out of my house when he misbehaves—one that teaches me daily about love, patience, and forgiveness.

How Easy It Had Been to Say Those Things Before Mission!

Courtney – El Salvador

In November, shortly after I arrived here, my fellow volunteers Ana Laura and Fabiane invited me to help them bathe a woman. I agreed, even though I had never bathed a grown woman before. As we approached the house, they explained to me that our friend, Niña Maria, was an elderly diabetic that needed help because it was just her and her husband, Don Javier, living in the house. When we entered the small room of their house, I could hear her crying from pain on the other side of the wall, which was a simple piece of wood dividing the room into two small separate rooms. Peering around the wall, I caught a glimpse of Niña Maria, lying naked on her bed, howling in pain. When asked why he had not taken his wife to the hospital, Don Javier replied through tears, "I can't afford it and a woman once went to the hospital and died."

It was the weekend; therefore Ana Laura, Thomas, and I came back on Monday, helped her into her clothes, put her in the wheelchair we have, and strolled her to the nearby clinic. The doctor gave her medicine for the parasites she had, and we began to check on her every few days. After Niña Maria had recovered, Ana Laura went to check on her and found her in pain once again. This time, she had broken her foot in two places. Our friend has a rather large belly and tiny legs that can't support her weight well, especially after being bedridden for a great deal of time. For months, we girls bathed her in her bed, and Thomas and Faby took her to her doctors' visits. When it came time for the removal of her cast, which kept getting postponed because her foot wasn't yet healed, we were all as full of joy as she was.

All of our friends were supportive throughout this difficult time. Crutches, milk, Depends, a walker, a new box spring, and other items were all donated to help Niña Maria. Faby and I began to visit Niña Maria and could now bathe her away from her bed. We became a tag-team, keeping Niña Maria laughing as we bathed her and washed her soiled clothes and sheets. So far, this has been one of the heaviest crosses we have been called to help carry. We often talk as a community about the difficult moments we had with Niña Maria and how they have helped us grow as a community.

There were moments where I was scrubbing her soiled laundry and wanted to flee the hot enclosed backroom of her house that was filled with strong unpleasant smells (our friend could not leave her bed and refused to use Depends). I prayed hard in these moments for strength and compassion. One day, I even thought to myself, "Okay. This is enough! Someone else can finish this project." I looked over and saw Fabiane graciously tending to Niña Maria's bedsores and reality hit. NO, we can't leave. She has no children. We are her friends. We are her family. We are it! My own words I used to describe my mission before I left for El Salvador started to echo in my head. "We do everything a friend would do. We give people back the dignity that has been lost." How easy it had been for me to say those things. To make promises. But, to live it, that is where faith, hope, and love truly come into play. Once I realized all of this, it became so much easier. It is love. Everything I do, I do for Him. At the end of every visit, she looks up at us, asks God to bless us, and gives us a big smile that shows off the gaps of her missing teeth. Now, I am the one introducing our friends to my other community members. But, every time she laughs, I'm brought back to that first moment that I was with Faby and she laughed the hardest I had ever heard her laugh. It was the first time we bathed her without her cast and away from her bed.

We Would Rather Treat Infected Feet

Kelsi – India

Once a month, we visit an area near the outskirts of town called "the dump." The people who live there are very poor, but there is always a strong sense of community. One day, as we were visiting our dear friend Mary, a group of young boys approached us. One of them was limping badly. Mary asked him why, and he showed her that he had a cut on the bottom of his foot that had become infected. We asked him if he had cleaned it, and he told us that he had nothing to clean it with and that he didn't know how, so we told him to come to our house and we would clean it for him.

The next day the boy arrived with one of his friends at 8:10 a.m. The boy with the cut told us his name was Tamil and the other boy was Parthiban. Parthiban then informed us that he also had a wound on his foot and asked if we could help him too. They, like most Indian kids, were not wearing shoes, so the condition of their feet and the wounds on them were less than appealing. We realized that we would have to wash the feet before treating them in any way, so I went to prepare some warm water and antibacterial soap. As I watched Latha and Chrisanne wash the feet of these boys, I was reminded of Jesus, who humbled Himself and knelt at the feet of His beloved friends to take them in His hands and to wash them.

We were behind on our weekly schedule and on this partic-ular day, we had planned on going to the market and doing the

105

cleaning and the planning and everything else that needed to be done, but when these boys came to our door with their dirty and wounded feet, we forgot about all of the things that we thought were so important and spent the entire morning caring for and getting to know Tamil and Parthiban, who we found to be two respectful, kind, intelligent, and very funny boys.

When they were well bandaged and ready to go, we sent them on their way with instructions on how to keep clean and told them to come back so we could make sure they were properly caring for themselves. As we were cleaning up and discussing the time we had spent with them, we realized that we would have to wait another day to do the things that we had planned on doing that morning, but more importantly, we realized that we didn't care. We were filled with joy and decided that we would rather treat infected foot wounds rather than complete our to-do list!

You Do This All for Me? But Why?

Natalie – Thailand

On this day, I was asked to spend the morning with Paa Nuaj, so that her teenage daughter (her now full-time caretaker) could go take an important test for her high school diploma. Paa Nuaj is a 57-year-old woman who suffers from diabetes and a number of related ailments. She can no longer walk, has recently been declared legally blind, and can do virtually nothing for herself anymore. She's lost a lot of her mental faculties as well. Her greatest sufferings, though, are spiritual and emotional. After a very broken childhood, she spent many years working as a prostitute in the slum, had a number of abortions, and has lived the past 15 or so years as a single mother of six children, the eldest of which is severely handicapped due to an attempted abortion, and two of which are currently in jail. The suffering of her tortured soul is almost tangible for me. Now that she can no longer go anywhere or see, she spends every day lying on the floor, alternating between sleeping, arguing with her daughter, and listening to the staticky reception of their broken TV. I used to really dread apostolate visits to her house because she repeats the same grudges, regrets, and anger over and over again, sometimes until she hyperventilates. Her world is so dark it scares me. Having spent more time with her and heard more of her story over this past year, though, I've been graced with a true friendship with her. While visits are still emotionally taxing, I do enjoy them now . . . and love her.

107

This day, after buying her some flowers after morning Mass, I arrived at her house to find her in the pile of trash in front of her house, with one of her legs wedged under the boards of her front porch. "Paa Nuaj! What happened?!?" I cried.

She was weeping. "Nam?? Is that you? I would have died if you hadn't come to save me. Maybe I should just die."

I spent the next 15 minutes or so in the trash heap with her, struggling and trying to dig her out. I'm glad she couldn't see that I was weeping too. It was physically (she's extremely overweight and had no strength of her own to contribute) and emotionally so much for me. I felt so small in front of her suffering soul. After getting her out, I helped her get to the bathroom and gave her a bath. Then I moved her to the house, dried her off, and put a diaper and clean clothes on her. She started to cry again, "You do this all for me? But why??"

"Because you're my friend, Paa Nuaj, and I love you." She nodded. She understood.

Paa Nuaj has become a part of my heart; that very heart where Christ descends to us on Christmas. It is into the trash heaps in my heart that Jesus *chooses* to be born. What attracts the Child is the swamp of misery and darkness. He wants to visit the place we think is untouchable. Paa Nuaj's cries to me are mine to Him, "I would have died if you hadn't come to save me" and, "You do this all for me? But why??" He comes to sit in our trash heaps with us, to dig us out, to clean us off, and to remind us, "Because I love you."

Chapter Six

I Was Tamed by My Rose

Someone to Watch Over Me

Marian – United States

This past Saturday, I experienced one of my most unforgettable encounters thus far. It struck me and will remain with me forever. I was walking through the fifth-floor corridor of a nursing home, when I heard, "HELP! HEEELP! HELP ME!!!" I could not ignore such a desperate cry. I entered the resident's room, not sure what I'd find. I saw an elderly woman lying on her bed, by the window, shades drawn. Her body was hunched into a most uncomfortable position, neck at a rakish angle, limbs wilted, her face angry, everything turned in on itself, and she incessantly screamed for help.

Sensing another's presence beside her, eyes still closed, she yelled vehemently, "I hate this! This stupid life. What the hell is the point? Just end this. My life stinks. Look at me. What am I doing here?" Her eyes were full of disgust, contempt, despondency. Such an open confession—her hatred for her life, her blatant cursing of her own existence. She cried out again, "HELP!"

"May I help you?" I said softly and timidly, not wanting to further ruffle her already very ruffled feathers.

She called me a few choice names. Then she opened her eyes just enough to look up at me. Her sinister expression fell with a sudden childlike shame. "Oh. I'm sorry. I'm sorry." She reached up for my hand. I took it and asked if I could sit beside her on her bed. She nodded yes, but she quickly returned to her inner cave. So, so dark.

"What are you doing here?" she asked me bitterly.

"I heard you calling for help so I came to see if I could help you."

"Are you here alone?"

"Yes. . . . Well, I got Jesus with me."

"Ahhh, Jesus. I don't believe in that." She pushed my hand and began to yell at me. I quickly stood up from her bed, afraid of what she might do.

I didn't blame her. Not one bit. I could understand. I sat beside her again. I just sat there. Soon she said, "I'm sorry." I assured her it was fine. She continued to tell me how meaningless and worthless she felt. I listened. She told me her legs hurt from being in the same position for so long. I asked if I could adjust her bed and pillows for her. She scowled as if to say, "What difference is it gonna make?" But she didn't say no, so I gently lowered the head of her bed and rearranged the pillows behind her sunken head. There. I felt like I could breathe a bit more easily just looking at her! Then I asked if I could massage her legs. She nodded yes. "Oh, that feels good."

"I'm hungry," she said. There was a package of doughnuts on her bedside table. I handed her one.

"I'm thirsty." Christ's cry from the Cross. There was a small cup of water on her bedside table. I handed it to her. A bit of the water ran down her chin, onto her chest. I wiped it off with a tissue. We sat together quietly.

I told her it was a beautiful evening outside. "Would you like to see it?"

She said yes. I was surprised and gladdened. I opened up her curtains. What a view! The Brooklyn brownstone rooftops were lit up by the late winter sun, slanted and brilliant. The sky was a bright, crisp blue.

"Isn't it beautiful?"

"Yes, it is," she said.

She was beginning to thaw out in the newly let-in warmth. I sat down beside her again.

"What is your name?"

Hearing no answer, I looked for it printed on her wrist band. As I saw it, she said, "Alice."

"Alice! I am Marian." I waited a bit. "I'm so glad to meet you."

"Oh, stop with that nonsense," she grumbled. I laughed with understanding. No warm-fuzzy social norms with this one! Love it. I moved to kneel beside her for better eye contact. She began to tell me about her life—that she lived in Brooklyn, was a good-looking lady with a good figure, was asked to be a model, and received a good education. She went to Brooklyn College.

"What did you study, Alice?"

"English lit."

"Do you have a favorite poem?"

"No."

"How about Robert Frost, 'Stopping by Woods on a Snowy Evening?'"

"I don't know it."

I recited it for her.

"That is lovely. A beautiful poem." Then she realized, "I do have a favorite song!"

"What is it?"

"'Someone to Watch Over Me.' Frank Sinatra."

"Ohhh! I love that song!" I sang the refrain.

She softened with recognition, "Yes, that's the one!"

I began singing the only verse I knew, "'I'm a little lamb who's lost in the wood'—How does it go?"

Alice chimed in, speaking the words slowly enough, line by line, for me to sing after her: "'I know I could, always be good, to one who'll watch over me. Although he may not be the man some girls think of as handsome, to my heart he carries the key. Won't you tell him please to put on some speed, follow my lead, oh, how I need someone to watch over me.'"

It was such a sweet sharing. She even let herself smile. A smile so precious to me.

She explained, "It's a nice song. But the words. The words really make it meaningful." She repeated with such earnestness from her own heart, "'I know I could, always be good, to one who'll watch over me. Although he may not be the man some girls think of as handsome, to my heart he carries the key. Won't you tell him please to put on some speed, follow my lead, oh, how I need someone to watch over me.'"

This is her heart's song, her cry. This is the help she was screaming for—someone to watch over her.

I gently took her hand and continued to sing to her, rubbing her arm. Her eyes closed peacefully. I sang her lullabies my mother sang to me. "Somewhere Over the Rainbow." "If I Loved You." She knew each one. "You could do this all day," she said contentedly. "Thank you for being here. You have a gift. A gift from God. To sing! Your voice is truly beautiful. Thank you for singing to me!"

"Oh, Alice, it is truly my joy. I could do this all day too."

"Now, don't make me cry!" she said. "Ya know, I always said, 'God gives us a deck of cards. We have to play it to the fullest!'" I smiled and thanked her.

I asked her if she knew "You'll Never Walk Alone." "When you walk through a storm, hold your head up high, and don't be afraid . . ."

". . . of the dark," she joined in . . .

Together, with her speaking and my singing: "At the end of the road is a golden sky and the"—

My voice broke.

We went on, ". . . sweet silver song of a lark. Walk on through the wind, walk on through the rain, though your dreams be tossed and blown. Walk on, walk on, with hope in your heart, and you'll never walk alone. You'll never walk alone."

I could feel each word pouring directly out of my heart into hers; or rather, being graciously spilled out over both of us like the sunlight through her window, seeping so tenderly into the curtain-enclosed rooms of our hearts. Really, Alice's cry is mine. Is ours. "Help! Somebody help me!" In our simple coming together, born from her honest, raw scream, there arose a solution—friendship. Such soothing ointment we shared in that moment. Each receiving, together, what we needed the most.

"May I come to visit you next Saturday?" I asked her.

"I would love that. Please do. You are always welcome."

"Alice, I love you."

"I love you, too."

I kissed her hand and cheek and said goodbye. "I'll never wash it again!" she exclaimed with a girly giggle. She took my hand and kissed it. Then she peacefully closed her eyes and dozed off into a calm rest, the sunset rays shining on her beautiful, serene face. I tiptoed slowly out of her room, not wanting to disturb the wash of peace. All was still and silent and gushing with a new rush of life. I was in awe and overflowing with joy and gratitude for having been part of a miracle. From darkness to sunlight, screaming to singing, loneliness to "someone to watch over me," despair to "you'll never walk alone." The miracle of friendship.

You Know My Home is Yours

Kelsey – Uruguay

Every friendship is a miracle, but the friendship with Sonia began with a particularly miraculous encounter. We had passed by Sonia various times in the *Costanera* seated with one of our friends, but she always seemed to be annoyed with us, questioning our mission and why we didn't serve food to the children as the volunteers that lived in our home years ago did. Her anger frustrated me, perhaps because her doubts about our mission were ones I once had in my heart. One day, Mathilde and I stopped to talk to Sonia in the middle of the *Costanera* and decided to stay and chat with her a bit longer. She began her usual rant and I tried to explain to her that our mission was of a different form; she did not understand. After all, friendship cannot be explained, it must be given, and it must be begged. Thus, I stopped trying to rationalize with her and asked her plainly, "But Sonia, do you consider us your friends?" This question changed everything.

"Yes, and you know that my home is yours," she responded. Wow. An incredible response, especially considering that we had never even seen her home . . . which I told her. She grabbed me by the arm and guided us to her home, a tin shack with a bed, a small kitchen, and not much more. She showed us the stuffed animals on her bed with much pride, and her joy filled the humble home. This hardened woman had become a small child showing us her home. She even invited us to return.

However, before we returned to Sonia's home, she arrived on our doorstep a few days later bearing gifts—a bag of flour to teach us how to make friend cakes (a tradition here), her old collected recipes (that she cherishes even though she cannot read), and a blank card for each of us—the treasures of her home. She stayed to drink *mate* and returned the next day to celebrate Mother's Day in our home, allowing us to get to know this mysterious child of God.

Sonia is a petite woman with a crooked trot, inviting you to link arms and walk arm in arm with her, with one eye fused shut making it seem that she is ever winking at you, and a laugh that fills the room and melts your heart. She has lived a long life, but one of much suffering, likely why she can be a bit rough at first. Yet after breaking through her barriers, she has a beautiful, pure heart that overflows with love. Despite many heartbreaks, Sonia continues to be a mother to her little neighbors, has rescued and cared for various neglected babies over the years, and seeks to help her pregnant neighbors. Her heart is enormous and now has fallen for us as well. She is a 60-something-year-old woman with the heart of a little girl and the faith of a true woman of God, reminding us, during a hard time in the neighborhood, "we do not live for this world, we are only passing by . . ."

No Tangible Needs?

Jennifer – Ukraine

One of our friends, Galina, asked us once, "Do you ever feel like you should be spending more time in the nursing homes or the orphanages, rather than with people like me, with students or with artists, or with average people? The people in the nursing homes and the children in the orphanages 'need' you so much more." I explained to her that at first, I did feel just that. There was a friend we often visited with whom I saw no "tangible" needs, and I wondered why we spent so much time with her. Then when something bad happened in her family, she called Con-solatio before anyone else. She wanted us. I ended up developing a very close relationship with her; she would ask me to spend a few nights with them at their house, or to run errands in town with her, or to watch her children while she went to the dentist. She expressed to me that she had no close friends and that she doesn't like living outside the city because there's not a social life. I realized that at first we don't see the reasons for the relationships we have, but always, always, God is nurturing and preparing those relationships for a reason—usually for a reason we do not see, and sometimes never see. Galina then explained that the reason she asked was because she realized that our door is always open, and that she "needs" the people at Con-solatio, that "many of us need Con-solatio more than we realize." When she wants to call someone to just talk or when she's sick, she thinks of Con-solatio. There are many souls and friends that are just as big of a part of our mission as those who are homeless, orphaned, or elderly.

I Was Struggling to Walk . . . and You Carried Me!

Regina – Ukraine

Since our visit to Kiev last month, my adventures have taken shape in quieter and more subtle forms. One particularly moving incident occurred following a gray week, on a lovely, sunny day. The sky was a clear, bright blue; the air was crisp and refreshing; and the whole city sparkled with ice. Maritchka and I strolled along on our way to visit a friend, chatting merrily. We stopped to peer in the window of the chocolate shop, see a couple taking wedding pictures, and admire the ice-coated trees glittering in the sun. We took a different route than I had taken previously, and I thank God we did. As we turned a corner, a strange and pitiful sight met our eyes. An old man was leaning on the weakest of trees for support as he attempted to use it to help him walk. It bent pathetically under his weight and merely turned him in a circle. Maritchka and I paused in our conversation as we passed and, at the same moment, both turned around and went over to him. "Can we help, *Pan?*" Maritchka asked. I'm not quite sure if he said yes, but Maritchka took hold of his arm anyway and I immediately followed suit, taking a firm grasp on his other arm. "Where do you live?" we asked him.

"Not far, just down the street there." We were going that way anyway. The process was slow going. The ice on the ground that had been a source of giggles as we slipped and slid along just moments before, now became a great peril. The man was weak and had pain when he walked, so we were forced to stop every

119

few steps. We both kept up a constant stream of encouragement, "*Давай!* Come on! You can do it. Just a bit further. That's it. *Давай!*" We finally made it to his home, and after he had thanked us for our assistance, we left. It was such a simple service that lasted all of five minutes and yet it made a lasting impression on me. The entire time I supported the man, these thoughts kept running through my mind, "This is Jesus!" and, *"I was hungry and you gave me food, in prison and you visited me, sick and you comforted me . . . . Whatever you do for the least of my people, you do unto me"* (Matt 25:35–40). There we were, two willing Simons of Cyrene, helping our Lord to carry His heavy cross before He died for us. I am so grateful that this beautiful moment was not lost on us.

Like All the Chains Were Shattered

David – Ecuador

This past Saturday, Matias and I visited the local drug rehabilitation clinic where we go every two weeks. It has anywhere
from 30–45 boys. The hardest part for the boys is that they aren't
allowed to leave the premises at all throughout the entire year.
No field trips, no extended lunch break, no vacation time. We
go to the clinic to offer them something different—a healing
friendship that's on their level. We go to get to know them, to be
alongside them in their loneliness or boredom or desire to talk
with someone who really listens, to be a presence of compassion
for them. What does this look like? Well, we never know until
we arrive. And we learn as we go.

That day, they were grouping into teams for soccer, and were
already inviting us to join two sides, when it started pouring rain!
In Ecuador, rain means that everything stops and everyone goes
inside. Just as we were accepting the reality that everyone was
probably going to want to go to their rooms to stay dry, a few
guys came sprinting out of nowhere and launched themselves
headfirst and shirtless onto the slippery concrete floor of the
soccer field, cheering and spraying a good 15 feet of rainwater
into the air with their stomachs. Woohoo! Yeah! A few guys came
right after them with the same trajectory. I thought to myself,
"Man! That looks like a lot of fun! But it's probably not good for
me to get soaking wet . . ." But then I thought, "What am I here
for?" So, I went for it. Ten solid feet! And I can't describe the

thrill of getting up, turning around, and watching Matias decide to do the same thing. It was like all the chains were shattered.

Our friendship with these guys will never be the same. The boys took the leap and Matias and I opened ourselves up enough to take the leap, too. To have shared something so silly, goofy, and adventurous as stomach tobogganing means that we're equals. We're from the same herd. We care about each other. It reminds me to pray for them as they each take the big step of getting over their fears and starting their lives over again when they return to their home environments.

Would You Give Us That Razor, Please?

Aaron — Argentina

We continue to make visits to the patients in Hospital Muñiz on Thursdays as a community. For the past three months, Tobias and I visited the patients with AIDS, but this past week we decided to start visiting the men in the tuberculosis ward, and our first encounter rather quickly confirmed God's providential guidance.

We spoke with a middle-aged man named César who, after some small talk and customary explanations about our mission, quickly began to share some of the difficulties and struggles in his life. His wife and daughter live in Ezeiza, about one hour south of the hospital, but they have not visited him, and it appears they do not intend to any time soon. César struggles with alcoholism and depression, and he has spent a bit of time recently wandering, literally and spiritually. "You two must be angels sent by God," he told us, "I was thinking about cutting myself again, but I think God knew I needed someone to talk to." He showed us the white scars and slash marks that covered the underside of his right arm and explained how he keeps a razor hidden under his pillow. We talked about his faith and his time in the hospital before we concluded the visit in prayer.

Before we left, I asked him to give us the razor. He grimaced at the request and stared blankly at his bed as he entered into an internal struggle. I reaffirmed that I asked this of him as a concerned friend and that this would be for his best to remove the temptation. After another pause, he agreed to give me the razor, which I later discarded with a prayer of thanksgiving to God. No doubt he will continue to struggle with his addiction, depression, and the temptation to despair, but I know that God is able to complete the good work he has begun in César. We hope to visit him again this coming Thursday, as well as our other friends at Muñiz.

More Than Just a Simple Paper Tossed into the Sea

Timothy — Peru

The first thing that struck me upon meeting Suzi was how often she mentioned how lonely she felt. The second visit was all the same. We talked about her grandfather, who had passed away a few years earlier, and then her uncle, who had passed away four months earlier. She told us how she had breakfast, lunch, and dinner alone when she wasn't out training to become a police officer or studying accounting at the university. She told us how her mother had packed up and moved to another city years earlier and started another family there. In tears, Suzi began to tell us about her loneliness and her ambition to secure her future with a career as a policewoman or accountant. She was determined, she said, to make something of her life and to get out of her current situation. Meanwhile, she said that her boyfriend discouraged her from training for the police and pursuing her studies at the university because he was jealous that she would meet someone else. She seemed to have everything going against her, except her determination to get ahead.

It was against this backdrop that one day, Suzi knocked upon our door, shortly after Alejandra and I had finished breakfast. I invited her in and the three of us began talking. She was completely burnt out and didn't know what to do. Recently, her mother had returned from Arequipa because her sister (15) had become pregnant. As a result, Suzi was now sharing her room not only with her mother and sister, but also her sister's boyfriend. This new living situation, on top of everything she was dealing with, left her completely overwhelmed. She didn't know where to go, what to do, how to act. In addition, her own boyfriend was pressuring her ever more to move in with him so that she could "free" herself from her family situation.

As it turned out, in the middle of our conversation, her boyfriend called her, and they argued a little over something or another and the tears began to fall. I went to look for some tissues as she hung up the phone. All she really wanted to do now was get out for a while and clear her head.

So, we prepared a backpack with all the necessary provisions and headed out to the beach. We didn't talk much on the bus. Instead, we sat silently and enjoyed watching the people and the buildings go by. There once was a time when I used to tell myself in these quiet moments that I should say or do something for the person that I was with, but I've since learned that the quiet is the quiet; it doesn't always need to be filled with conversation or activity. Just being there is enough. When there's something to be said or done, it will come naturally as did the conversation we had that morning as well as the decision to head to the beach.

About an hour later, we arrived at our destination. We spread out the blanket and enjoyed the experience of sitting by the ocean. Yet this was not the reason we had come. Rather, during our conversation that morning Suzi had mentioned that she wanted to write out all her feelings, stress, and confusion onto a piece of paper and throw it into the ocean. So, after we had lunch, I handed her a pen and paper so that she could get to it.

Once Suzi finished, she crumpled up the letter into a ball and tossed it into the ocean. However, because of the wind, it hardly made it more than 15 feet, only about halfway to the water. So, I stood up and retrieved her crumpled note and helped her wrap it around a rock so she could try again, which she did with success. You could see in her eyes that she was relieved. Perhaps not so much for having thrown a piece of paper into the ocean, but rather, for the time spent away from the stress in her life which gave her a chance to think about her direction, her goals, and her desires, and to put everything in order.

On the way back, we prayed the Rosary together on the bus. There, she was able to pray for her family and for the grace to overcome the challenges in her life. We knew that certainly she would face difficult times ahead, but right then, that was okay. What she needed that day was simply a peaceful moment shared with people who listened and who really cared about who she is and what she was going through.

Not the "Lightning Bolt" Sort of Way

Katie – United States

I have been struck often in these past few months by how much my life is made up of very little things. Answering the phone (it rings off the hook some days!), inviting someone over for a cup of coffee, remembering to call and sing "Happy Birthday" to a friend. Last month, it was something as small as making valentines.

Every week, Joanna and I visit a homeless shelter here in our neighborhood. Everyone there is struggling with burdens that I can't imagine, with labels that seem stuck forever, and with constant reminders that they are on the margins of society. As we've been trying to be faithful in simply showing up each week, we are always looking for ways to open up these simple encounters into deeper friendships. In this age of instant gratification, I'm often unaware how much I want this to happen right away, in a dramatic, "lightning bolt" sort of way. But love, *real love*, takes a lot of simply showing up for the little things.

So, we invited a few of these women over to our house to make valentines for our elderly friends at the nursing home. Of course, we didn't plan on it being the coldest day in New York City in a hundred years! Even though the cold kept some people away, there were a few brave souls who made it, even bringing a friend at the last minute. At first, everyone looked at me a little funny when I suggested making valentines with Bible verses about love. Then someone found the glitter, and suddenly we were kids again—cutting out red hearts on construction paper and making glitter hearts and gluing on sparkles! Suddenly it wasn't about us, and we were thinking about who would receive these valentines and what they said inside, *"For I am convinced that neither death, nor life, nor present things, nor future things nor any other creature will be able to separate us from the love of God in Christ Jesus our Lord."* (Romans 8:38) At the end, I heard someone say, "Wow, it's been so long since I've done something like this. It's nice to do something beautiful for someone else, and to be here in such a peaceful place." Isn't that how the best friendships start—with the little things?

The Only Way to See Rightly

Christine – Romania

Before you read this letter, you should first search the Internet for "Chapter 21" from the book *The Little Prince*. It's a (very short!) story about a meeting that the Little Prince has with a fox. During this meeting, the fox explains to the Little Prince what it means to "tame" him, saying that the Prince should come every day at the same time to sit near him. Every day the Prince should sit a little closer to the fox, until eventually the fox is no longer afraid of the Prince and they can be friends. The fox also tells the Little Prince that once they have "tamed" each other, they will be unique to each other. The Prince realizes this is true about a rose that he has "tamed." When he looks at other normal roses, he says, "You are beautiful, but you are empty [. . .] One could not die for you. To be sure, an ordinary passerby would think that my rose looked just like you—the rose that belongs to me. But in herself alone she is more important than all the hundreds of you other roses . . ." Before the Little Prince leaves, the fox tells him a secret that too many people have forgotten, "It is only with the heart that one can see rightly; what is essential is invisible to the eye."

I read this story about a month ago, because we depicted this story in a play with a group of kids while they were staying at our house for a camp that we put on for them. The first time I read it, I immediately thought of one of my close friends here, Margareta, who is a 28-year-old woman with a mental handicap.

She grew up in an orphanage because her family was too poor to care for her. She has two children who are cared for by a loving family here in Deva. She is unmarried and homeless. Her family and her occasional boyfriends have only ever tried taking advantage of her, and since she knows this, she has left all these people behind. Due to her mental handicap, she sometimes becomes angry easily, and while she is an incredibly gentle human being, she often speaks aggressively.

Throughout my time here, I've gotten to know Margareta very well during our long walks to the Social Services building, to the hospital, and to the town hall to resolve one issue or another with health or government aid. I comforted her when the homeless shelter told her that she had exceeded the number of days that the law permits her to stay there. I went with her to print photos from her birthday party that we threw for her and laughed with her as she showed me the photos over and over and over again as she reminisced about that beautiful day. I was with her at the hospital when she needed to get rabies vaccine injections after a dog bit her leg. She came with us in our apostolate to visit a gypsy community, which she pronounced to be just like Africa. She spent hours working in our garden with us and helped us make about 15kg of strawberry jam. Just as the Little Prince "tamed" and was "tamed" by his rose and his fox, we too began to "tame" each other and after a few months, I realized that I love this woman to pieces. She has become unbelievably important to me and incredibly close to my heart.

This past month, I've spent even more time with Margareta, since we have been helping her through the process of obtaining the housing that she is entitled to, due to the fact that her mental handicap prevents her from working. About a week ago, we received amazing news: a room had become available for her in the one of the housing projects! She would no longer have to sleep in the woods nor store her small bag of personal items at our home for safe-keeping. She could clean herself and make her own food. We were ecstatic for her when we heard the news, and Margareta herself was so overcome with joy, she began telling every single person she came in contact with that she *finally* had a room all to herself, where she could sleep all day if she wanted to without anyone bothering her.

However, when we arrived at her little room, I felt as though someone had dumped a bucket of water on the flame of my joy. Her room didn't meet the standards that we were hoping she would be able to have. Also, through the process of moving her into her room, we came into contact with too many people that spoke with and looked at her as though she was an animal. My heart burned with anger and my eyes burned with tears the entire day. How could they treat her that way? Margareta . . . *my* Margareta. Why couldn't they see what I see in her: a gentle, honest woman, full of love and hope, who speaks everything that's in her head and on her heart?

It took me some time to remember that I looked at her the same way when I first arrived in Deva, and I have no doubt that if I had never gotten to know Margareta so personally, I would have continued to look at her in exactly the same way. It is no more than a grace and a gift from God that I can see Margareta for the incredible human being she is, full of the dignity and beauty that He created inside each of us. I can't judge anyone for how they see or treat Margareta. Every person who doesn't know her is only an "ordinary passerby" to whom Margareta is a rose just like any other. I can only get on my knees and thank God that He blessed me with such a friend as her—that He gave me the opportunity to allow her to become more important to me, "than all the hundreds of [. . .] other roses: because it is she that I have watered; because it is she that I have put under the glass globe;

because it is she that I have sheltered behind the screen; because it is for her that I have killed the caterpillars [. . .]; because it is she that I have listened to, when she grumbled, or boasted, or even sometimes when she said nothing. Because she is *my* rose."

Margareta has "tamed" me, and I have "tamed" her. She is now unique to me in all the world. I thank God that I can see her with my heart, and not just with my eyes. "It is only with the heart that one can see rightly."

Chapter Seven
Led by the Lowly Ones

A Dignity that Nothing Could Remove

Regina – Ukraine

Pan Petro is my inspiration whenever we walk into his room. When he was 13 years old he stepped on a land mine which exploded, leaving him with only one working arm and two shriveled legs. One half of his face is disfigured, and he was blinded by the incident as well. Yet there is a dignity about him that nothing could remove. The first time I met him, I was amazed at his words, "I am so grateful for each day God has gifted me." He spends his days moving his fingers over his rosary beads, praying to Our Lady. One day, when we came into his room, Pan Petro was the image of weakness. He was slumped against his pillows and his voice was slurred and unclear as he prayed. But when we asked him if he was tired, he replied, "With God, I am never tired." Why? I wonder. What makes him rejoice in God in such a deep way? What gives him this strength to love his simple and difficult life? So many would turn against God, blaming Him and even begging for death, but Pan Petro, in his quiet dignity, accepts all.

"Wasted" Perfume

Anna – Brazil

One encounter that keeps coming back to me happened just about a month ago with Ana. Ana is a middle-aged woman I absolutely adore. She suffers greatly from schizophrenia, but somehow she manages to live on her own. One day we were talking about traditional breakfast foods in our native countries. Here in Brazil, a normal breakfast is made up of rolls, *cuscus* (boiled corn meal), eggs, coffee, and juice. When we asked Ana what she typically eats she replied, "I can only afford a piece of bread in the mornings, and an egg when I can afford it." We continued talking.

"Hey Ana," I said, "I'm thirsty, would you mind bringing me a glass of water?"

Without hesitation she jumped up and asked, "Sure, but how about tea? Or maybe you would prefer coffee? Do you want coffee?" A few minutes later, she excused herself and ran out the door to a nearby store. When she returned, she was carrying the ingredients she needed to make me some juice. This woman who cannot usually afford so much as an egg with her breakfast, without giving it a second thought, desired to give us the very BEST she could without stopping to count the cost!

Upon reflecting on this encounter with one of the other volunteers, we were reminded of Mary who anointed Jesus' feet with the finest perfume and wiped His feet with her hair. *"Some of the people there became angry and said to one another, 'What was the use of wasting the perfume? It could have been sold for more than three*

138

hundred silver coins and the money given to the poor!' And they criticized her harshly. But Jesus said, 'Leave her alone, why are you bothering her? She has done a fine and beautiful thing for me. You will always have the poor with you, and any time you want to, you can help them, but you will not always have me. And she did what she could,'" (Mark 14:4). Just like Mary, Ana has a love for us that does not count the cost, a love that immediately desires to give the best of oneself and what one has for the other.

In the Heart of a Garbage Dump

Sofia – Senegal

Walking with Ibrahima through the little shanty town that has been set up in the heart of the Mbeubeus dump felt like walking through a small town with one of its beloved members. Ibrahima greeted people right and left, making comments as we went along, "That guy is a good man. That is a good friend of mine. He doesn't get into trouble."

Being the good host he is, Ibrahima introduced us to the village chief, whom we found lounging majestically in his home, a circus-sized tent with carpeting made of mismatched fabrics and large tires as chairs. We then met Ibrahima's friend Mohammed, whom Ibrahima considers the greatest inventor in Mbeubeus. Mohammed's makeshift home has a workshop, numerous bedrooms, two bathrooms, a kitchen and even a small garden. "My first home was even better than this one, but it burnt down a while ago because of a fire in the kitchen," he explained. Right when I was starting to think how awful it must have been to lose his shelter here at Mbeubeus, Mohammed quickly added, "But God is good."

Ibrahima got very serious and added, "We must thank God for everything. He has created everything. Breathing: God! Eating: God! . . . All the mysteries in life we can thank God for." I was moved by Mohammed and Ibrahima's expressions of dependence and gratefulness; I could see that it brings lasting peace to their daily lives.

Good Eating and Passion Sharing

Brittany – Ecuador

We organized a cultural dinner for some close friends of ours in the neighborhood. What is a cultural dinner? Well, it is a night of good eatin' and passion sharin'. Everyone invited to the dinner was asked to present their passions, their gifts, their interests. The theme? Beauty Will Save the World. The point? To encourage and inspire.

The dinner was meant to encourage our friends to appreciate that they each have something special to offer others, some gift they can share, and to figure out what it is. The dinner was meant to inspire our friends with the various beautiful facets of life: food, art, nature, creativity, friendship, etc.

It all began with Julia and her mom (who was visiting from Austria) presenting their mutual love for cooking via a traditional Austrian dish for us all to enjoy. Next, *Señora* Tanya shared her talent for making baby clothes. *Señora* Naycli humbly presented her knitted treasures and many hand-made bows. *Señora* Nancy modeled the women's clothing she sews. *Señora Ester* gave us a step-by-step cooking lesson for baking a chocolate cake from scratch. And the best part was we got to eat it afterwards!

From our community, Philippine presented the drawings of the Ecuadorian artist Oswaldo Guayasamin—famous for depicting the sufferings of the Indigenous peoples. Finally, I brought my love of nature to our living room by organizing a slideshow presentation of the various natural landscapes found in Ecuador. To encourage and to inspire. Beauty will save the world!

141

The Freedom of Real Love

Jessica – Senegal

My friend Adama is a 16-year-old girl who lives in Malika. She comes from a family rich in love and children but poor financially. My friendship with Adama has developed in a very natural and genuine way throughout the course of my time here.

Adama is the third oldest in her family and the oldest daughter still living with her parents, so like most Senegalese girls, she takes a lot of responsibility with the five younger children and around the house. One of her younger siblings is a boy named Lamine, who is handicapped with a problem where his muscles don't fully develop. Thus, he requires a lot of care and attention, none of which he is lacking in his extremely loving family and especially from Adama. It's evident from spending the smallest amount of time with this family that there is a lot of love holding them together.

In my last letter, I spoke to you of *L'Abri*, the center for children who are handicapped where my friend Antoinette lives. Since the school is run through donations, we suggested that the family send Lamine in order to receive medical and professional help for living with his handicap. The transition has been difficult for the whole family but especially for Adama and Lamine, simply because they're so close that it's hard to be apart.

When Lamine is on vacation from school, we normally help the family to pick up Lamine from school. Lamine is normally extremely upset when vacation time ends and expresses his distress in a manner that is sometimes revolting. I recently accompanied Adama with a knowing and sad Lamine back to *L'Abri*. In the bus, his normal smile had diminished into a blank stare with his lips curved downward. I saw the pain on Adama's face as her brother suffered. We began to talk, and she told me how she knows that he will cry soon and that she will too after. She also told me that despite it being hard, she knows that Lamine's going to *L'Abri* is what is best for him and that gives her the strength to accompany him back. It's obvious from this last remark that she is completely mature in her love for Lamine, and really is such an example of what real love is—not possession, but freedom.

Lamine started crying the moment we left the bus, knowing what neighborhood we were in. Not even Adama could comfort him as he clenched her shoulders. So obviously, I could do nothing to comfort him either. I could just be there with them, at the foot of the cross of their suffering and offer my hand to walk with them. After an extremely difficult goodbye full of expressed anguish, Adama and I started to walk together back to the bus stop. I saw the tears in her eyes and knew how heavy her heart was, making my own heart heavy and my own eyes fill with tears. In my helplessness, all I could do was keep my arm around her shoulders. After a while, Adama turned, looked to me with a huge smile, and asked, "What's wrong?! Why are you so sad?!" I stared back at her awestruck while realizing that she was not faking that she was okay. We talked about how it's almost a grace for it to be difficult for Lamine to go back to *L'Abri*, because it means that he's really loved by his family. So many children don't have this kind of love, and so many people don't know the kind of love that Adama and Lamine know. It's real love, and she's taught me so much about it.

A Seed of Attraction

Brittany — Ecuador

Oh, the kids. I love these kids so much, but during the *permanencia* (when we open our doors to the kids from 3–6 p.m. every day), the needs can be overwhelming. Many days during the *permanencia* I will have a little one in my arms, while another is asking to be picked up, right as Anita asks for water, while at the same time two kids ask for paper so they can draw, exactly when Alejandro begins to cry because someone hit him . . . and then the phone rings. The kids that come to the *permanencia* are the kids that normally spend all day unsupervised in the streets. There are a thousand signs that make me believe they are not well cared for. They hit and yell and don't know another way to communicate. Many have bruises and scars and when I ask what happened, they say, "I fell." But they look at me with vulnerable and lying eyes. I know they did not really fall.

The kids come to our house to be loved. They come to be heard. They come to play. They come to be in a place where they are important and are shown "another way." They come to get the attention and direction that all kids need.

Rodo, the youngest of four boys, is one of the kids that is faithful in coming to the *permanencia* nearly every day for a break from roaming the streets. At four years old, Rodo is normally quite loving and adorable, but recently, Rodo suddenly took a turn for the worse and began biting, hitting, yelling, and being overall rebellious. When I had to tell him to leave the *permanencia* for his disruptive behavior, he sat outside on our front doorstep quietly thinking for the remainder of the *permanencia*.

A week later, an outdoor Mass was celebrated on the side of our house to give a blessing to the prayer garden we constructed (the intention of the garden was to inspire our neighbors with the beauty of nature and to encourage prayer with the image of the Blessed Virgin Mary holding the young King Jesus.) Rodo came to the outdoor Mass . . . and brought his mother. This day Rodo was fascinated with the Mass. After communion, he said, "What was that they put in your mouth? Open your mouth! Let me see!"

"It is Jesus," I said.

The next week when I was closing up the *permanencia*, Rodo found out we were going to Mass and asked, "Why don't you take me with you?" Ten minutes later, Rodo showed back up at our house with his "nice pants," two sizes too big and strung up with a belt, with permission from his mom to go to Mass with us. Hand in hand, off we went. This night was one of my favorites that I have lived thus far in Ecuador, with this precious boy at my side. I had never seen him behave so well. If I knelt, he knelt. If I stood, he stood. He has asked to go to Mass with us four times this past week. Four times he has gone.

The other day he even colored a picture (appropriately in blue) for me to give to the Virgin Mary! It fills me with hope to think that perhaps a seed of attraction to holy things has been planted deep within Rodo, a seed that will mark a transforming path for his life.

Her Home-Made Wall

Marie-Celeste – Thailand

Until now, I had never realized that I operated by the rule, "if at first you don't succeed, pick yourself up and try again." Of course, this made perfect sense to me; I'm new to this whole mission thing, so I don't know what I'm doing. I will fall so I will have to get up again. In general, this was a good plan, but as my time here was growing, so was the number of falls. I found myself trying to operate by a new rule "if I never fall, I never have to embarrass myself by trying to stand up again" or "if I keep my falls to myself, then I don't have to bother someone else with helping me get up again." This fear of failure placed an unreasonable demand on me.

How can I possibly share mercy with anyone if it is something that I don't allow myself to experience? Here the children have taught me a new rule, and it is simple. In fact, all that they do is add on to the end of all things, "and, I love you."

I fall down, and I love you.

I stand up, and I love you.

I do it all again, and I love you.

I just broke your nice coloring pencils, someone peed on the floor, pick me up, and I love you.

There is a little one named Duwee, who is a frequenter of our house. She is a wiry eight-year-old, who prides herself in her ability to do her own braids (which often come straight out of her head like antennas) and the small pink and green purse (carrying a chopstick, old cell phone and a few *baht*) that she wears across her chest and gets tangled in her arms, as she loves to be flipped. Duwee doesn't have many friends, and she has developed toughness from being made fun of by the other children. One of her favorite stances consists of crossing her arms, jutting her jaw out, cocking a hip and looking you toughly right in the eyes. I think of this pose as a home-made wall, built up in the hopes that if she manages to look strong, the harsh words will somehow not be able to enter and hurt her anymore. Sadly, I see a similar "toughening" in many of our friends. What, then, is the role of a volunteer of compassion, of a friend? What if we were able to fan the little ember in her heart that still feels, that wants to nurture and be a blessing rather than to lash out or shut down?

One morning, Duwee joined us for breakfast at home. We were all laughing about something, and seeing that the laughter was dying out, Duwee attempted to carry on the good times with a joke used on her too often, *"Phii! Phii Maye Suaye!* Hey Big Sisters! You aren't beautiful!" Now, how do you add on "and, I love you!" to that? Seeing that she wouldn't be getting the response she had hoped for, she began to close up quickly, but not quickly enough as you could see the small hope in her eyes that we wouldn't yell or hurt her back for her unkind words.

The only thing we did was offer Duwee a "Do-Over" as my mother calls it, a chance to completely start again, without any stain or holding-over of her mistake, a chance to experience mercy. For Duwee, this was the most radical and unexpected thing we could do. Not only did she open back up, but there was a new blossoming in her heart that we'd never seen before. It was lovely.

"Sometimes a thing needs to be reminded of its loveliness . . . and the soul quickens at hearing what it didn't know it already knew."
— Gregory Boyle, S.J.

Neither the Forest nor Disneyland

Mara — Ecuador

Do you remember when I wrote in my very first letter about a field trip we had taken some of the neighborhood boys on? Well, we just had the opportunity to do it again! Only this time, instead of a big city park, we took them to a forest preserve. There, instead of a lake to jump into, there were monkeys and birds to be watched during a three-hour hike. The experience this year for me was very different from the field trip last year; firstly, and most obviously, because I now speak Spanish well and thus had a little more of a grip on the situation (hallelujah), but secondly because I have spent over a year getting to know these boys, their stories, their suffering, their joys. My gaze toward these boys has been transformed, and I now see more clearly their childlike hearts and beautiful qualities, often hidden beneath their street-hardened attitudes.

The outings we go on with these boys serve as a concrete way to manifest our love for them and to expand their horizons farther than the streets where they spend their days. Through the time we spend with them, they slowly realize that, with us, they are looked at differently, they are treated differently; we offer them something more which they don't find easily elsewhere. I saw them come alive with simple, innocent, childlike joy. Pablo started singing Christmas songs as we tramped through the forest, changing the words to make them more suitable for a hike; Andres spilled over with smiles on the big carousel swing at the end of the trail; several of them almost took off enthusiastically into the brambles to look for the monkeys we could hear through the trees, marveling at the beauty and wildness of the great outdoors that they seldom experience. At the end of the day, I couldn't help thinking, "why do we have to take them back? They are much better off here." How easy it is to think that way! However, looking at them, I realized that rather than trying to escape the suffering that reality presents us with, our consolation is found in Christ who took on flesh, entered our human reality, and redeemed suffering once and for all. For these boys, their happiness is not found in the streets, nor the forest, nor in Disneyland. It is found in Christ, and my job is to lead them to Him by loving them as He loves.

Saint John Paul II says, "Life with Christ is a wonderful adventure." I can attest to that—during this year I have done many things that I never imagined I would, accompanied by many "How did I end up here?" moments, shaking my head and grinning at the Lord's sense of humor.

Their Tiny Lives Teach Us

Erica — Brazil

Helena and I arrive at school by 8:30 and all the beautiful children greet me with hugs. They call me *"profesora de arte."*

Now that I have become more accustomed to the rhythm, I find teaching much more enjoyable. We laugh all day. I love to play jokes with the kids, and I have become more familiar with their idiosyncrasies. Mateo is in love with Claudia and if I look away, he kisses her arm or leaves the room to get her water. When I reprimand him, he replies, "but she really likes me." Adriano is about a foot and a half taller than I am and cannot fit in the regular desks, so he uses the teacher's desk. He does not follow directions and normally manages to work for about five minutes before he becomes concerned about the rosary that hangs on my arm that he wants to belong to him. Cristiano is a wonderful artist, but if I don't switch out his paper often, he gets bored and falls asleep. He likes his backpack to be hung from the desk perfectly and often rearranges the things inside, which include his toothpaste that he likes to show me. Cristiano wants to marry Rafaela, who sits quietly in the same desk each day. She waits patiently for me to help her with the activities and then continues until I return to help her stop. If I forget, which happens often, she will paint or color the entire page.

Last week Rafaela surprised me because when I walked into the classroom, she reached out her arms to me. I had never seen her make a movement alone and it caught me off guard. She smiled. I kissed her head. Then walking to the bus, she uttered in this tiny, beautiful voice that I had never had the pleasure to hear, "Bye."

Anita does exactly what she is asked and is the classroom police. She tells me *all day* who is burping and not covering their mouth, who went to get water without asking, who is talking too loudly, etc. She sits in disdain of the others. I love her. Then Carolina laughs all day. She gets so excited about every little thing and tries to put the materials in her backpack. She loves to show the other teachers her work even though she barely manages to do any of it. She is very sensitive to touch and loves to hold and kiss hands. Felipe gets angry with me more than once per day. He is always blowing me kisses and does not like to listen to me. He gets stuck on something he wants and if I don't give it to him, like two sheets of paper instead of one, he cannot do any work. There are others, of course, and there are many other classes as well.

I was thinking the other day how our children here must be saints. They teach us so much. Each one of them suffers from the tragedies of their lives and each of them expresses it differently. Yet, they teach me about my relationship with Christ; they teach me about love and patience and forgiveness and joy. They are the chosen ones and I thank God for them. For this, I think their prayers reach His ears more quickly, and so know that we pray for you and God hears them.

Didn't I Have Better Things to Do?

Kelsi – India

As Latha and I walked down the street one sweltering, Indian day, we heard an all too familiar little voice yell, "Heeeey!" We scanned the horizon and sifted through the scenery of cows, cars, and people until we spotted him: Rajesh. Our favorite little terror!

Rajesh is 11 years old and is afflicted with a slight mental handicap. The good Lord has bestowed on our little Rajesh more energy and willpower than anyone knows what to do with. He can be difficult to handle at times, but we love him dearly and he never lets us pass without a hug or an affectionate bite on the arm.

On this particular day, after waiting in the heat for a bus that never came and walking to the other side of town, I inwardly cringed at the delighted little "heeeey" of our beloved Rajesh. "We'll stay for a few minutes then tell him we'll come back another day," I told myself. But, as usual, Rajesh and God had other plans in mind for the afternoon. So, it came to be that Latha and I (after Herculean efforts to dissuade him) departed for destinations unknown with Rajesh leading the way.

To be honest, I was a little annoyed by the fact that I was being dragged up a hill by an 11-year-old boy because, after all, didn't I have "better things to do?" However, soon after these thoughts crossed my mind I realized where we were going. He was taking us to Calvary Mountain. It is a peaceful little hill adorned with the Stations of the Cross, statues of Jesus and Mary, and a small meditation chapel.

When we reached the top of the hill, he led us to a statue of Mother Mary holding Jesus after the crucifixion. I was deeply moved when Rajesh approached the image with childlike reverence and tenderly placed his right hand on Our Mother as she cradled the body of her lifeless son. He placed his left hand on his chest and bowed his head in silent prayer and at that moment everything made sense to me and my anger turned into wonder.

I realized then that God uses the smallest and most unlikely means to lead me back to what is most important . . . to lead me back to Him. I think He wanted to remind me that I really don't have "better things to do" because my journey toward Him is the most important thing in my life. I never thought that this little friend of mine would be so instrumental in my journey because, once again, I underestimated God and the people around me.

The remainder of our time was spent on Calvary Mountain. This time, as I looked into those big black eyes and took the small brown hand that is forever ready to hold mine, I did it with a smile on my face and joy in my heart.

Chapter Eight

Here, at the Foot
of the Cross

Tending to Our Wounded Humanity

Jessica – Senegal

At the beginning of Holy Week, we received a call from Khadi's son to tell us that she was really, really sick. Khadi has been friends with our community for 21 years, since the very beginning. She currently lives in Malika, the neighborhood that we visit that's next to Mbeubeus, the garbage dump. Khadi works at Mbeubeus, doing extremely difficult labor for hardly any salary. I worked with her one day for only a few hours, and I can't imagine how she works this way every day. Khadi is probably one of our friends that suffers the most for a variety of reasons: marriage/family-wise, financially, and also from loneliness. When she's sick, there's no one who takes care of her, so we invited her to rest at our house for a week.

She arrived Wednesday night in complete physical suffering. Her entire body hurting and tired, she couldn't do much but leave her bed. I started to suffer myself at seeing this woman that I knew already suffers so much in the state she was in. I began to pray and took charge of giving her all of her numerous medicines throughout the day. Therefore, I spent a lot of time with her, and I was really touched by the trust that started to build from this relationship. It's true that the way to build a friendship is through fidelity.

On Good Friday, the day of the passion of Christ, Khadi was also suffering a sort of passion. Throughout the day, I would walk into her room and find her body hot with fever and her groaning in pain. In the evening, Charlotte and I gave her a massage with mint leaves to try and help her relax her tired muscles a bit. As I was massaging her feet and legs and Charlotte her shoulders, Charlotte remarked, "You know, I was a bit sad all day because Jesus (in the Eucharist) isn't in the chapel. But then I realized that He's just outside the chapel," gesturing to Khadi. That's it! That's exactly it. In this moment, I realized my mission more clearly than ever: tending to the wounded Christ, our wounded humanity.

Khadi is better now. Keeping in rhythm with Jesus, she was better by Easter Sunday. Even she said in Wolof, "I was healed on the feast of Jesus. He resurrected, and I resurrected too." Even though not Christian herself, she saw this parallel. Easter was beautiful. Khadi dressed in a beautiful *BouBou* and even danced. I was filled with such immense joy at seeing my friend dance and being able to dance alongside of her to the traditional Senegalese rhythms. After that, we were able to enjoy four days of Easter joy with Khadi at our house, completely renewed. At one moment after crying, she said, "Without my Con-solatio friends, I think I would have already died. Because of you and your real friendship, I am not alone."

On a Bitter Street, a Sweet Truth

Katie – El Salvador

I have waited so long to write this particular letter—it needed lots of prayer and the right words, because what I want to share is about a place of bitterness. That's what people call it here: *la calle de la amargura* (the street of bitterness). It is a place we, just the women of our community, go to visit every Tuesday afternoon. Just off the main road, in a neighborhood not far from our house, are streets lined with open rooms and bars, full of women scantily dressed, waiting. Waiting for the next customer who will humiliate them even further, as they try to sell the only thing they seem to have left—their bodies. It is not an easy place for me to visit—I have to let go of a lot of my preconceptions in order to visit friends here in this place so "godforsaken." Yet it is here that I spend the most time talking about God!

Niña Rita, a woman close to my mother's age, is the owner of a bar here. She is usually dressed up, with every accessory coordinated and wearing a lot of jewelry, when she welcomes us back to the quieter part of her bar to chat. After offering us a cool drink, we chat—about everything and nothing, and I find myself charmed by this kind, intelligent woman. Then . . . we pray together. I am always struck by the simplicity and truth of Niña Rita's prayer. No matter what evangelists in the street yelling God's condemnation say, or how long she's lived bound up in this life, she knows that she is the beloved daughter of God. We are simply there to help her remember that.

It's probably Niña Rita's prayers that helped our friend Gina to finally quit her work in the bar and find a better life for herself and her children, and what's helping our friend Cynthia to tell us more often that she is tired of this life. I remember when I first met Cynthia she was reading a Jules Verne book and we talked about our favorite books together. She's a soft-spoken, gentle woman with an obviously quick mind and big heart. I wonder often how she ended up in a place like this. She talks to us most often about her kids. She worries about them, prays for them, wants a good life for them. Now that they are almost grown, the economic pressure that forced her into prostitution has eased a little and the other kinds of work that she can sometimes find seem more possible. She dreams of owning her own *pupusería* (to sell yummy *pupusas!*) and of finding a man who will truly love her. She knows that she is more than her work, more than her label, more than all her past mistakes.

It is not always easy to visit friends here, because alongside the joy of encountering these beautiful women is the powerlessness that I constantly feel in front of their suffering. Ironically enough, it is here, on the margins of "respectable" society, that I find those most ready to hear the good news that they are inherently worthy, full of dignity and beauty. Why is it that I struggle so often to remember this truth about my own dignity? That I, broken and wounded in so many ways, am loved because of who I am, and not what I do. It is my friends here on this bitter street who are teaching me the sweetest truth.

Not a Conventional Happy Ending . . . but Worth Living!

Gabriella – Honduras

A few weeks ago, I found one of my *"bolito"* (drunkard) friends, Felipe, seated in a shady spot. As I approached him, I realized that he was crying—definitely not something you'd want to do if you don't want to be made a target of cruel jokes and teasing. With a simple, "What's going on, Felipe?" he answers equally as simply, "I've been real sad these days." He goes on to tell me that he has nowhere to sleep at night, he usually finds the bed of a pickup truck to spend the night, his entire family has left the neighborhood, and he has nothing to eat or to do. He continues saying that maybe it would just be easier for everyone, himself included, to find a way to end his life. I assured him, "Felipe, you know how sad that would make me, how sad it would make many here in the neighborhood. There are people here who care about you."

The alcoholism here in our neighborhood is rampant, perhaps a consequence of the incredible unemployment and the vicious cycle that starts with the young people who witness and live with alcohol in their families as children. The *bolitos* are regularly depreciated, insulted, and told they are losers and useless for the trouble they cause. They are not completely without fault, but just the same, the humility of their profound desires is found after taking just a couple minutes of my day to put aside my reservations, ask how things are going, and sincerely listen. Beneath the dirty words, the belligerent fights, the demanding requests for food and money, and the shady deals they get themselves into to make a few *lempiras* to buy their alcohol, they suffer for the same reasons as the rest of us. They are lonely; they feel like what they are doing is useless; they want someone to love them unconditionally. Having so little, they are so grateful for the simple respect and concern we show for them. Forming friendships with the *bolitos*, my heart breaks for them more than almost anyone else. For many, I see no exit from this path that leads to nowhere, and I feel impotent to do anything to improve their situation. I sincerely suffer with this hopelessness with the *bolitos*, but also with other friends of ours: the old folks in the *asilo* who are simply waiting out their last days; the women in the jail who have been there for 10 years and still have 20 to go; the young people who see no prospect for employment after they graduate from high school; the mothers who spend more time working to make ends meet than raising their kids, and then don't know what to do when their kids enter a gang; and the families who are separated from their loved ones who have left for the US or Spain to work.

Perhaps I don't suffer in the same way as my friends, but it is the part of my mission that tests me, the part of my mission that isn't so pleasant. Not all of the stories have a happy ending, but it is in this suffering of mine that I find compassion—literally "to suffer with." Letting myself assume some of the suffering of my friends, I begin to really love them. I look back at my year and a half here, and many things are the same. The *bolitos* still drink, the people are still unemployed, the gangs still exist, the heartbreaking violence never ends, the young people still leave for the US to work, and there are still people who have nothing to eat. The difference is that I love these people, and they love me, and because of that, all of these sad stories that perhaps don't have a conventional "happy ending" are worth living, and we find a way to be happy together because of the love we share. This is the miracle that God gives us: the ability to find this profound joy in the midst of the day-to-day sufferings that we share.

A Deep Enough Silence

Katie – United States

The other day a friend asked if I could go with her for her che-
motherapy treatment. I had no idea what a lesson it would be for
me in how to bear the Cross. She is in her late 70s, distinguished
and "full of wisdom" as the Scriptures say, full of that astonishing
capacity to quietly accept deep suffering, which I often find in my
older friends. When I arrived at her house, she was weak and short
of breath, so we didn't say much on the ride over to the clinic.
The nurse who welcomed us was kind and patient, explaining
every step of the procedure and bringing warm blankets for my
friend. At first, I didn't know if she wanted me to chat with her
or not, and she seemed so tired that finally I realized she just
wanted to rest as much as possible. There wasn't much I could do
to make her comfortable, nor much she asked for—it was simply
a matter of me being attentive to her and waiting. She didn't turn
on the TV, so I read a book for a little while, and then began to
pray the Rosary. After a while, I could see she wasn't able to rest
because her legs were bothering her, so I offered to read to her
to "distract" her, but she said, "No thanks, even though my legs
are bothering me, I'm trying to pray . . ."

So, we waited and we prayed and there fell between us a
silence that was . . . *true* somehow: a silence deep enough to hold
her long struggle with cancer (this is her second bout with it);
deep enough to let her rest from the well-intentioned friends
whose chatter had exhausted her; deep enough for me to see

her faith "strong and sure as a Lebanon cedar" which is carrying her through this valley of the shadow of death. It was a silence long enough for me to remember that my words are so often unnecessary, here at the foot of the Cross. Long enough for me to be aware that what she needed from me was for me to carry her in prayer, to offer quietly and discreetly my attentiveness. That what she absolutely didn't need was my fussing over her and chatter to distract her. *"Though I walk through the valley of the shadow of death, I will fear no evil, for you are with me."* (Psalm 23:4)

One Last Intense Gaze

Lenore – Ecuador

We had the blessing of meeting Rosa about two months ago, when her cousin told us how ill she was with cancer, and we promptly went to visit her. Only 35 years old with a three-year-old son, she was extremely ill, incredibly thin, and barely able to eat. These past two months have truly been a journey with her, as we witnessed and accompanied her in the ups and downs of the illness. There were days when she improved and could sit up and talk and other days when she was completely exhausted and barely conscious, lying in the bed. Each Sunday, we would bring her the Blessed Sacrament and despite her illness, it was one of the most beautiful things to witness the reverent and humble way in which she received the Eucharist. On Palm Sunday, Mike and I had the blessing of going to visit her, and she was in very good health. That week, she was going to enter SOLCA (a cancer research hospital) to receive treatment and we had a beautiful conversation with her and her husband about her illness, suffering, struggling spiritually with her illness, the Faith, and the grace of God in this time of suffering.

About two weeks later, I was visiting near her home when Carolina found me and told me that Rosa was dying, so that I could go visit her. What a blessing! When I entered her now familiar room, I was shocked by the drastic change in her. While she had always been petite, she seemed a shadow of herself, so incredibly thin and delicate, unable to eat or speak, and suffering great pain but surprisingly still lucid. I knelt down at her side, took her hand, and simply offered up a prayer with her that she might know the consolation of Our Lady in this moment. Although her face would become distorted with pain at times, she made an effort to look at me and acknowledge my presence with her, and not so much that it was me that was at her side, but that I was representing the presence of our Con-solatio community with her at this time. I had to leave her, but by the providential design of God, as I was walking home, I encountered our parish priest who was coming to give her the Last Rites and asked that I lead him to her home. So, I had the great blessing of accompanying Father Pedro to her home and, together with the family, witnessing the moment when he gave her the Viaticum. One moment was particularly moving: I happened to look upon the face of her husband as he gazed at her . . . and I have truthfully never seen such suffering, such inexpressible pain, a face that seemed to be crying out for mercy to be able to support living through these last hours and moments. As I left with Father Pedro, Rosa gave me one last intense gaze . . . and the whole scene became a Golgotha for me.

For me, it was an immense grace that continues to humble me and for which I can only profoundly thank God that I could be at Rosa's side, stand at the foot of her Cross, be present at this Golgotha in the most concrete sense, and like Our Lady, seek to be a silent presence of compassion and love, which is at the very heart of our mission.

When There Is No Silver Lining

Anna — Brazil

It was Saturday morning. I was in the middle of cooking lunch when Dina entered the house. She has four kids, two of whom live at the *Fazenda* because she is unable to care for them adequately. (The *Fazenda* is a farm where our volunteers live and welcome children and other people in need of a refuge and a fresh start.) As she sat down, she gave us some disturbing news: her ex-husband had been murdered the night before. It was such a shock. "Oh, what am I going to say? How do I explain to my children that their father was killed?" In my mind, all I could think was, "God, isn't their life hard enough?" Their family lives in a small, cement, one-room home. Since her husband left, there has been no stable male presence in the house, and now this. It is in moments like this that I'm stopped dead in my tracks, blocked by a reality that is too big, too difficult to face. This reality is how little control we truly have in our lives. I would love to believe there is a silver lining to every storm for my friends here, but this is just not the case for a lot of them. My hardest work is done in Adoration every day where I am forced to look at Christ and utter one of the most challenging prayers, "Lord, even if things go terribly wrong or don't improve, I choose to trust you." With another deep breath, I pray, "Your will be done." My friends, in trials God sows the seeds of trust. A great consolation for me is that this family doesn't have to work through this alone, we will be at their side every step of the way.

If You Have No One Else in the World . . .
You Have Us

Kelsi — India

To bathe a grown person can be a scary thing for an inexperienced person. To bathe a very old person with leprosy and a broken foot borders on terrifying, but, one fine morning Chrisanne, Latha, and I set out to do just that.

When we arrived at the room of Pathamma, she was in the same place and position that she had been in the day before. She had not moved in some time and was lying in days' worth of her own waste. Near her head sat a bowl of untouched food. The hum of flies surrounding her unmoving form was audible. There were ants in her mouth.

We were seized with pity for this woman who had long since been abandoned by her family because of her illness. No one cared for her. No one loved her. This human being, this soul, this supreme creation of God was left alone to wallow in the degradation that had befallen her, and not a single person cared. Filled with the compassion of Christ, we boldly proclaimed, "We will care for you. And if you have no one else in the world . . . you have us."

Girded with the armor of prayer, we stormed the gates of this woman's personal hell, willing to do everything in our power to alleviate her misery, even if just a little bit for just a little while. We had next to nothing in the way of supplies but made do with what was available to us. We asked her neighbors to lend a few things, a pot to heat the water, a wall to hang the saree to dry. None of them was very fond of her, so it wasn't easy, but we managed to scrounge up what we needed and then got to work. We washed her saree, cleaned her room, and then came the hard part . . . bathing Pathamma.

We suspect that she hadn't been eating or drinking for a while and as a result, she was a little out of it. I think she didn't have the energy or the presence of mind to speak to us. She said a few words of refusal when I tried to feed her, but that was about it. While we were bathing her, she reached up and began to wash her own face and at that moment, she gave us a smile as bright as the sun. Then, just before we left, she clasped her hands in front of her face in a silent gesture of gratitude. Those two actions, as small as they may seem, meant more to me than a thousand thank-yous.

We told Pathamma that we would return and we told ourselves that, next time, we would be better prepared. That was the last time I saw her alive, though. She died just a few days later alone, and in the same state in which we had found her. When we came to pray over her before the burial, we were dismayed to find that even in death, she was uncared for. Her family was notified, but no one came, so only the bare minimum was done for her and I can tell you that for a lonely leper lady, it isn't much. There was nothing I could do to change it, so I tried my best to accept it. Her funeral consisted of Father John, Latha, Chrisanne, a few men who also had leprosy, and myself. It was very short and very simple.

After the funeral, one man approached us and thanked us for the work we had done for her. He said that after we helped her, other people took notice and started to do little things for her also. In saying this, he showed us something that we very rarely, if

169

ever, get to see. He showed us the fruits of our mission. Not only had we brought compassion to this poor woman, but it touched those around her also. In some way, by providing us with the opportunity to see this grace, Pathamma gave us a much greater gift than we ever could have given her.

How Can These Walls Contain So Much Pain?

Natalie — Thailand

The Immigration Detention Center (IDC) is a place of unimaginable, overwhelming suffering—the heat, the smells, the being stuck in a dark concrete cell with up to a hundred other people, the anguish of loneliness, the lack of solutions, and the seeming hopelessness of anything better for so many. Every time I visit, my senses and my heart are bombarded, and I'm left wondering how the walls can contain so much physical, mental, and emotional pain. The IDC is intended to be a temporary place (hence the word "detention") where those without a valid Thai visa are held as they await the money and paperwork to be sent to another country.

At any given time, 800–1,000 individuals from around the world—men, women, and children—live together among the 15 rooms in Bangkok's IDC. Over the years, through our twice-weekly visits, we've befriended many of them: each with a different story, all with tremendous suffering. We rotate visiting each of the large rooms, and those thirsting for friendship will come to encounter us at the room's one barred window.

As I reflect on what I "do" at the IDC, I realize that most of it comes down to small gestures packed with attention and intention, meant to convey the love of God. All stems from and relies on prayer. I cry with the asylum seeker who realizes he will probably never be granted refugee status or see his wife and children again; I hold the hand of a woman who has been in the IDC for

171

five years and cannot speak the same language as anyone in her room, but understands and smiles when I tell her she is beautiful; I jump for joy when someone shares that he received the funds to go home; I listen attentively to the talkative man with mental illness who tells the same stories every week, while the other men in his room roll their eyes and laugh at him; I look into the eyes and massage the hand of the woman who has lost her mental faculties after many years and can no longer speak; I bow to the prisoners belonging to a race seen as "below human" by some other groups in the building; I hug the children and spin them around on their way to the IDC "school"; I try to listen intently and respectfully to the ramblings of the schizophrenic woman who is (rightfully) feared by the other women and children in her room; I sing and pray with a group of women and exchange hand kisses as we part.

One woman there has taught me more about compassion than I've learned anywhere else in my life. She is stuck in the IDC as she waits for refugee status. Her life is in danger in her home country, where she is well-known for her speaking out against violence and oppression of women. Here in the IDC, you can see that same spirit driving her, as she takes young prisoners and the outcasts of the room under her wing. She once thanked me for our visits and said, "You remind us that we are human, and are not forgotten." I hope so. She and I have had some beautiful conversations about the voice of God throughout her journey, and they always bring me to tears. I asked her if she had written anything that she wouldn't mind sharing with me, and that I could share with others as a means for them to meet God. Here is part of a journal entry she gave me in response:

The wisdom of God has ordered the paths of prophets in the Bible in those days; this is the same wisdom that is ordering our lives today. . . . Therefore, we shouldn't be discouraged when unexpected and upsetting situations come our way as a Christian—it means God in His wisdom wants to make something of us. . . . Who knows? Maybe when our cross becomes heavy, God is teaching us how to be patient, or He is breaking our pride in order to live in humility and have compassion . . . I just praise God for all these bad experiences . . . there is a way God is leading me . . .

In the IDC room, there is one mentally disordered woman from Vietnam. At the beginning, she was aggressive. One day she fell very sick, and there was nobody to take care of her. During that period, she had saliva all over her body because of the injection and medicine they have given her—she could not control her movements, her mouth was opened and so the saliva was everywhere. Everybody was running away from her as she was smelling bad. God gave me love and compassion for her. I used to wash her and clean her place and wash her clothes every day. I was sharing my food with her, but she could not eat so I used to buy milk for her. That was a very difficult period. People were despising her. The day I decided to bring her to sleep in my bed, people shut their mouths and stood amazed; I was happy that night to sleep on the floor and to let her rest. I saw her, she slept like a baby. I praise God that that period has passed.

She has started to get back to normal little by little; it's my prayer that God will heal her completely. . . . Somebody has shown me love today— my Vietnam girl, in her state, has brought me food . . . she cannot speak English, I cannot speak Vietnamese, we just communicate with our hearts. The girl, after a while, she brought me most of the things she received! I was shocked and refused to take, but she just kept bringing . . . I saw love in her eyes! She was happy to offer me something. To make her happy I just took a small pack of noodles and gave back to her as she needs it more than me. My girl knows I love her. She knows that when nobody was there for her, God showed her love. Oh, I remember those days, every time I take her in the bathroom for shower, since she could not move, I started to wash her body. She always had tears in her eyes—only God knows why she always had tears. . . . I always cry when I see the love of God for me—and I think: only God can be with me in this particular circumstance. The grace of God . . . the Love of God!!

On His First Day of Freedom

If you read my last letter, you may remember a young man I spoke about whom we visit in one of the local jails, *Kuya* Julius. Well, after 11 long years in jail—11 years Julius describes as God breaking and transforming his hardened heart to draw him closer to Himself—his sentence was dropped and he was released. Con-solatio volunteers have been visiting Julius and following his case for years; many past volunteers have become close friends with Julius through their visits and even have continued to write to him after mission. Many have been praying for his release, as evidence seemed to prove his innocence, and yet the process has been long and complicated, and at times it has seemed he would never be released.

I cannot then begin to tell you how exciting it was when on the night of March 27, when we were praying the Stations of the Cross, we heard someone call at the door and came down to see Julius standing there with his sister and little niece and nephew and a huge smile on his face. He had been released that morning and was completing a list of things he had planned to do on his first day of freedom. First of all, family was so important to Julius, and in jail he often expressed his desire upon release to continue his education if possible and to find a job to help support them. It was important for him first to see his family. He wanted to visit the grave of his mother, the only one who would consistently visit him in his first years of prison, but who passed away during this time. He loved her very much and would pray for her often; in his cell he kept a picture of her which he surrounded with beautiful flowers that he had constructed with materials given to him in prison. It was also important for him to go to church to thank God for all He has done for him. Finally, he wanted to visit us. Now here he was, after a long day of freedom coming to be with us and to thank us for our friendship, for our presence in his life during his 11 years of imprisonment. I cannot express how overjoyed we were to see him and what an honor it was to have him show up at our house on his first day free.

He joined us in the chapel that night to finish the Stations of the Cross and then we did what only seemed fitting to do—we had a pre-Easter celebration. Eleven years in prison, coming out at the age of 30, this young man truly has experienced God's mercy in a radical way. Similar to the story of the prodigal son, Julius was, *"dead, and is alive again; he was lost and has been found,"* (Luke 15:24). In a way, he is a symbol of Christ's death and resurrection. Christ died with him to raise him up. Again, Julius was not found to be responsible for the murder he had been convicted of, but according to Julius, he was still far from God at this time in his life and he was grateful to God for now giving him a chance to live a better life outside of jail, one rooted in Him.

Since the night of his release, we have continued to stay in touch with Julius and always love when he surprises us and stops by. I ask that you continue to keep him in your prayers now more than ever—that he can stay strong in the midst of all his new trials and reentry to life outside of prison, and that if it is God's will, he may continue his studies or find a less burdensome job. He has come back to a difficult and broken family situation, and his dreams for education have been put on hold.

In his readiness to work, he has lost no time in finding a job, but it is a very difficult and tiring job unloading the transported rice from the ships. We have seen him a few nights completely exhausted from his work. It is amazing, however, to see how he continues to love his family even when this love may not always be received; how he accepts his work however difficult it may be. And that above all he continues to trust in God.

Never "Why Me?," Always "Take Me"

Renee – India

In her five years living at the Garden of Mercy, Victoria witnessed to everyone the spirit of our mission. This petite young woman came to the Garden at a time when she was completely estranged from her family . . . and very soon she knew she had found her true family. I saw her every week when I came to the Garden for my day of rest. She often kept me company beside the sewing machine as I stitched new clothes for my fellow volunteers or for Victoria herself. As soon as she knew I could sew, she was making her requests and even involving me in her bag business. I accompanied her one day to the association where she learned this bag making trade. She wanted me to learn how to make the lining for a specific bag and then teach her so she could improve the quality of her creation.

There were moments of joy and laughter as we unpacked the lunch she prepared, and moments of sadness as she told me all her sorrows on the train . . . questioning the meaning of her life. Yet her consistent quest for beauty was Victoria's key to life. She revealed beauty in everything around her from the flowers in her garden which she would proudly show me and then gather for the chapel, to the brightly colored bags she would knot for hours on end, happily adding her own personal touches . . . even in the tasty sweet treats she would conjure up and serve with giggles.

Around May, our dear friend Victoria, who was suffering from AIDS, began to get very sick. The whole summer she was in and out of several hospitals and care centers, returning to her home at the Garden of Mercy weaker each time. It was beautiful to witness the tender love and careful attention of each volunteer taking care of her in her last days . . . trying with all their energy to give her hope to fight and to survive. Victoria was free . . . and for those spending day and night at her bedside in the dingy old hospital, this freedom was difficult to bear. All we wanted was for her to live, and after 28 years of suffering, Victoria wanted to go home to the God she loved. On the dreary afternoon of August 17, I was at the foot of the cross of Victoria as she drew her last breath and put herself into the hands of God. My fellow volunteer Marguerite and I remained at her side in prayer and adoration, knowing through our tears that she was finally released from her suffering . . . and that her life did have meaning.

God revealed to me a deeper meaning that beckoned me to go beyond her suffering for what it was . . . and soon I looked at her struggle to keep living as an endless prayer . . . as an offering for the salvation of the world, uniting her passion with Christ's. Her life gave me meaning and the courage to live the life I have been given. For Victoria never said, "Why me?" but always, "Take me."

Seemingly Frail and Weak

Francesca — Romania

Her mouth moved slowly again, and she started to share. "It happened last year, at an empty train station. It's hard to say." She ate another bite of spaghetti, her long spindly fingers twisting the fork against the plate. Her face was thin. Too thin. She swallowed, and the story tumbled out.

"When I went home, my mom didn't believe me. She wouldn't call an ambulance—that would shame the family. So, I went to the hospital on my own. Everyone talked. I didn't say anything. Who would believe me? Only my aunt believed me." She wiped her mouth with a napkin, which did nothing to remove the orange stain from her lips. There was a pause. "I want to go back, but I'm scared to go back. To the train station, I mean."

She looked at her phone. A message from her new boyfriend. Apparently, they'd been together a month now. She opened the message and smiled weakly, a forced smile that didn't reach her eyes. Her eyes never smiled. "He just broke up with me."

My first reaction was to be angry at God. What cruel timing. Then I was angry at myself for making assumptions about her life before I'd taken the time to listen. This girl, so seemingly frail and weak, was in fact stronger than most girls I know. She had been betrayed by someone she trusted, and then kicked out of her own home. She had moved to Deva to continue going to school, where she suffered vicious rumors about her morality, and was now working ungodly hours with a bully of a boss in order to support herself.

None of us knew what to say. We were all racking our brains for the appropriate response to such a traumatic story followed by an untimely breakup. This young woman was sitting before us having just opened up, her heart raw and hurting. The silence stretched on. That's when it came to me: what to say. It came just like that, as if God had waited until my heart was knocked off its pedestal and stinging from humiliation to prove that in my sin and weakness His power is made perfect. So, I started sharing what God had placed on my heart, opening up about my own experiences, and before I knew it, we were having a conversation, a real conversation.

When we got up to leave, I told her I would call her.

"Call me," she said, timidly looking me in the eye. "No one ever calls me to see how I am."

Her response caught me off guard. I had meant I would just call to schedule another lunch date, but her eyes were so blue, so tired, so hurt. She was thin. Too thin. "Yeah, for sure," I said and smiled. She gave me a hug and walked away.

What If This Is Where You Want Me?

Mayra – Brazil

I met her on my very first week of mission. We walked toward a tiny house that was guarded by three noisy dogs. We saw Dona Gloria from a distance, sitting at the entrance of her house. A 72-year-old lady elegantly holding a cigarette with one hand while the other one rested on top of her crossed legs. She was wearing a small, white dress that made her white, freckled skin and white, curly hair even brighter. She had quite an attitude, very strong, yet she had sweet and comforting words: "Have you talked to your mom already? Make sure you let her know you are okay. Moms worry, you know. Come visit me, I can't go out of the house as much as I used to, so you come and visit me." I heard many stories about Dona Gloria and her visits to our house; she used to say that she had a "quite happy and entertaining life" (with a mischievous smile on her face). She was a free spirit, never settled down with a husband and had only one son with whom she chose not to live. She loved her freedom.

One day, her neighbor came to our house letting us know that she had fallen and was taken to the hospital. We called her son and told him what had happened. Two days later, as we were coming back from our retreat, we decided to go straight to the hospital to visit her. To our surprise, we found out that in fact Dona Gloria had been in the hospital for four days and no one had come to see her other than her neighbor the second day she was there. She was in a corner of one of the big cold emergency rooms, naked and halfway covered by a sheet that didn't do much to keep her warm. A plastic bag with her clothes inside served as a pillow and her paper bag was at the foot of her bed. She used that as a purse and carried it with her everywhere with her most important belongings. She had broken her hip and had a lung infection. The lady from social services looked at us a bit upset and said, "Are you responsible for her? Do you know she has been waiting here to be transferred to a hospital downtown but needs someone to sign and do the paperwork?"

We explained to her the situation and we all kept trying to call her son. When we finally got a hold of him, he said, "I can't go now, I work far away. I will be there tomorrow night. She probably just fell like she has many other times."

I couldn't believe it! I was full of so much anger. How could someone just leave his mother in the hospital like that? She was so weak, barely talked. We stayed there, holding her hand, caressing her head, and letting her know we were there for her. Without expecting an answer, we said out loud, "We are going to pray the Rosary now, Dona Gloria." She suddenly opened her big, blue eyes and looked into our eyes as if she was trying to understand what was going on. We got so excited! "Do you know who we are, Dona Gloria?" She nodded. "Were you waiting for us, Grandma?" She nodded again.

After a couple of minutes, she said a bit impatiently, "Let's do it!" We looked at each other confused, and then we realized she was talking about the Rosary. After we were done praying, she said, "It's done." She held our hands very tight. At one point, she hugged Hortencia and did not want to let go of her. We decided then that we had to stay with her until her son arrived. Hortencia would stay until the night, I would stay overnight, and Ana would come the next morning. It was hard to leave the hospital; she would not let go of my hand. She was so cold and kept saying,

"It's done. Time to go." Just half an hour after Ana and I left the hospital, Hortencia called us and said, "She died. She just died."

We called her son to give him the news. After some silence, he said, "I'll be there in about an hour," and hung up. I thought to myself, "NOW you can make it? Now that she is dead? She waited four days for you, and you didn't make time for her!" The next morning, we woke up early and went with him to get Dona Gloria ready for the burial. I thought relatives would come to help as well, but to my surprise it was just him outside the funeral home. The three of us, along with him, carried the casket to the cemetery across the street. As we placed it in a small stone chapel, the man in charge of the cemetery asked, "So, what time do you want the burial at?"

The son answered, "Now is okay." We looked at each other confused. He noticed our confusion and he just said, "No one else is coming." We asked him to please give us two hours to gather a few friends from the neighborhood that would want to be there for her burial and pray the Rosary. He agreed and so Ana and Hortencia went to gather the people while I went to get candles and a couple of flowers. When I got back, I saw something that will stay in my mind forever, as it crushed my walls of judgment and criticism. A man all alone, crying, hugging the casket of his mother. The echo of his cry filled the emptiness of the small chapel and it felt as if my heart had stopped, as if time had stopped. I could actually *feel* his pain . . . . Reality hit after a few seconds, and I didn't know what to do. "Should I stay, should I give him some time alone? If I stay, what do I tell him? But what if this is where You want me? Oh God, oh God, oh God!!"

He suddenly turned to me with his face covered in tears and just kept repeating, "I didn't know, I didn't know it was that bad." We sat next to each other and then he started telling me, "You know, I am her only son. So many times she drank, fell, went to the hospital and I had to be looking after her. I lost so many jobs. I asked her to come live with me, I asked her to stop drinking!"

Truth is, no one really knows what happened to Dona Gloria, no one knows who took her to the hospital or how she fell. "Someone just heard it from someone."

That week I couldn't help but to think how blind I can be to the pain and suffering of the ones around me when I give room in my heart for judgment, my own life experiences, or very superficial glances of "reality." How hard is it for God to see His children struggle to find this love that He offers so abundantly and freely?

I am blinded most of the time; sadly I have to admit it.

But not You. You see us the way we truly are.

For a couple of seconds, You let me see through Your eyes.

My heart becomes flesh. Is it pain or it is happiness that I feel?

And somehow, I can understand You a bit more.

I can see why You would send Your only Son.

I can see why the Son would give His life.

Time keeps passing by and death becomes a wakeup call for those who stay, a call to live, to truly live and experience life to its fullest. "What am I here for?" Well, that one week, an old woman didn't die alone in a hospital. A man didn't cry alone upon the death of his mother.

Chapter Nine

I, Too, Want to
Join the Feast

One Day, I Will Go Back!

Mayra – Brazil

Imagine an old church in the middle of the chaotic city fish market and cargo ship port. The big, rusted gates at the entrance open to a stair that leads to what was once an imposing, white church. This is now the home of many who at one point ended up living on the streets. In the middle of the deteriorated yet beautiful church, each one finds a corner to place a piece of cardboard and sleep. Anyone who passes by the church wouldn't dare to enter; no one would think that inside there is a beautiful garden with many handmade decorations. Paintings, flowers, and carved statues lighted by candles give the prayer time held there a sense of tranquility and communion. I guess this place is just like our friends; many pass them by, rejecting their presence because of how they look, and in the process they miss out on the beauty that each one has inside.

The day of our visit was Thursday: the day in which the community welcomes any homeless person who would like to have a moment of prayer. After the celebration, we all have dinner and share together about life. As Mateus and I walked into the church, we saw a couple of people already inside. Two of them had found a comfortable corner and were taking a nap. There was a guy sitting by himself in the circle of chairs that had been prepared for the night celebration. His face was a mixture of relief and fatigue at the same time.

"Hey there! How are you?" I asked and he looked at us a bit lost. "I'm so sorry! Did I interrupt your prayer? We can come back later," I said.

To my surprise he replied enthusiastically, "No, no! Please stay!" as he straightened on his seat and pointed us to the chairs next to him. The nervousness and happiness with which he embraced our presence melted my heart.

The introductory questions are usually the same, yet the history, experience, suffering, and happiness of the answers of each person amaze me every time. "What's your name? How did you get here? How old are you?" . . . and so on.

"My name is Alex and I've been living on the streets a bit over a year. I heard about this place through another organization. I like it. It's nice to have a place to sleep and not worry about the rain, the mice, someone stealing the little you have, and, boy, do I love the dinner and that prayer time!" He kept talking about his life on the streets: the fights, the friendships, all the unknown beautiful places of the city. "I could give you the best tour of the city and I'm not even from here." We were excited to see the enthusiasm with which he was telling his stories, and so we kept asking him questions. We learned how to take a bath by the ocean by digging a hole in the sand and also how to properly secure your belongings before you fall asleep on the street. Yet there was still this question in my heart, the question that I'm sure many of us have when we see someone sleeping under the bridge of a fancy city, or asking for money in the plaza's corner: "Why are you living on the street?"

I had never asked that question directly of anyone, but Alex was being so open and honest about his life that the question popped up naturally after he talked about his family back in the interior of the state.

"Why are you living on the streets? Why don't you move back with them?" I asked, and a shadow covered his face, a mixture of embarrassment and reflection.

"I've hurt too many people," he said and after a quick, profound silence he added, "You know how people tell you, 'don't do it, it's hard to get out of there once you are in.' Well, I didn't listen. I thought I was strong enough. Drugs. Crack. Look where it has taken me." A sad smile was drawn on his face and he said in a hopeful tone, "I want to go back. One day I'll go back. I don't know what I will say to them, but I'll go back."

I've heard the parable of the prodigal son many times, but somehow my heart just kept the "happy ending." The son who repents and comes back ashamed to his father's house. He is welcomed with arms wide open, and a feast is made in thanksgiving for his return.

How much courage does it take to go back? What would you say to those you have hurt? Afraid of rejection, ashamed for what has been done.

Father, I have sinned against heaven and before you. I am no longer worthy to be called your son. (Luke 15:21)

How to repay? What will my punishment be?

"Treat me as one of your hired servants." (Luke 15:19)

I have lied . . .

I have stolen . . .

I have cheated on my wife/husband . . .

I have ended life in my womb . . .

I have beaten, insulted, criticized . . .

I have hurt so many people . . .

"I would do so many things differently in my life if I had a chance to go back in time," Alex said.

"The fact that you have learned from what you have done is a great step. Many don't even realize what they have done and continue to live in a lie. You do have a chance to go back, not in time, but to give your testimony and help those who could be following the same path you did," I said in a poor attempt to lift him up.

The sound of steps approaching the circle of chairs interrupted our conversation. The night prayer was about to start. He didn't sit next to us, so when the time to greet each other in peace came, I started looking for him around the big circle. I found him on the other side, and he seemed to be doing the same thing. I waited as his eyes traveled through the crowd and finally met mine. The smile on his face right after that moment was beautiful. I walked toward him in between the crowd that was giving and receiving hugs and my arms finally reached him. The hug didn't last more than four seconds; however, that simple gesture echoed in my heart for much longer than that.

I have questioned the parable of the prodigal son many times (even after the countless explanations). Why a feast after he comes back? Now the happiness of the Father has touched my heart, and I, too, want to join the feast! The words that come out of a repentant heart fills mine with so much joy that I just want to make a feast out of it.

"My son was dead, and is alive again; he was lost, and is found!" (Luke 15:24)

The wrongdoings are no longer important; the punishment is not even thought of.

"There will be more rejoicing in heaven over one sinner who repents than over ninety-nine righteous persons who do not need to repent." (Luke 15:7)

So They Can Learn to See Themselves with New Eyes

Anna — Peru

The metal door grates behind us and then slams shut, the padlock clicking into place. We are met by a round of applause, a communally shouted greeting, and a sea of eyes of about 70 boys that have turned to see who has entered. The boys are scattered about a concrete patio, hanging out along the edges, joking around with each other, staring out into space, singing with the music from the loudspeaker. We walk up to a few, and then they begin to come, and the drilling of questions starts . . . What is your favorite Peruvian food? What were the streets like after the World Cup soccer game last week? Where do your eyes come from? They are so blue! Are you scared of me? If you saw me on the street, would you recognize me? You know that the only thing we see of the outside world are the planes overhead? How am I supposed to change? What would you have done if you were in my situation?

One of our weekly apostolates is a rehabilitation center for about 700 boys around ages 14 to 20 who have committed some crime. Every week, two people from our community go to visit the center. Originally, it was not easy for me to enter into the world behind the walls, and I often went bracing myself for the conversations of the day. I may have entered through the doors of the building, but I did not let the walls of my heart fall down. I did not want to let them in; I just wanted to survive my hours there.

Yet I knew that Christ was there. I knew that there was brokenness there. I just didn't want to confront it. After several months, I went for the first time to visit the *"Bienvenida"* (Welcome) patio, where everyone goes when they first arrive. They stay for a month, awaiting their sentence and patio destination. There, I saw the raw reality—the boys in their frailty and fear, before being toughened up by the daily drudgery of life in the center. Some boys lying curled up on the concrete floor, sleeping. Others spending all of their hours making origami paper creations to pass the time. Others in silence in the corner. Others joking loudly with the boys. All of them in waiting. They are quick to share their stories.

"Ramon got here two days ago—he's been sleeping there the whole time."

"They got me on my way home from school . . . . The police pulled up alongside me, showed me a picture of my face and told me to get in the car . . . . I didn't have time to let my family know. I still don't know if they know where I am, and I've been here for a month. They might let me go soon, or I might have to stay several years—I just have to wait to see what they tell me."

"My one-year-old is left with my girlfriend, who often is off partying."

Here, all the snippets of conversations started to come together. My walls began to crumble, and I saw them not with fear, but with a deep, deep sadness. As little boys, lost, trapped within their worlds—of peers, drugs, pressures, desire for "manliness," not knowing how to escape. Once they leave the center, they enter into another encasement—that of their past lives, mistakes, and bruises that have led them to such a vulnerable state and labeled with the name "prisoner." The question stays in my head: What would you have done?

Now when I enter the rehabilitation center, I am washed over by the deep hunger of each of these boys to be seen as a person, not as his act or crime or label. I have begun to think maybe that's why we go there—to see the boys differently than most people look at them. To look at them as someone's son, someone's brother, someone's father—someone loved. To see them as Christ, who also was once a prisoner. To recognize God's gaze upon them—one of mercy and love. So that they, too, can learn to see themselves with new eyes.

Until I Saw His Eyes!

Emily – Argentina

A few months ago, I became friends with a man who has dramatically marked my views on life and on my mission here. Let's call him Carlos. Carlos was born into a rich family in the mountains of Paraguay and spent more than a few decades of his life like St. Augustine. That is to say: a lot of alcohol, money, and women. Eventually he wound up here in Buenos Aires and spiraled downward into deep poverty. His long-time lady companion left him for another man with more money and he stayed behind, completely and utterly alone. He fell into alcoholism and took up a few jobs here and there, and started going to the soup kitchen to survive. His health became very poor, and he could hardly walk, let alone work.

The first time I went to his house, I knew what to expect. I had been warned. We knocked on the door as usual and waited. You could hear the slow shuffle of someone walking stiffly inside. The curtain was pushed aside slowly, and I was face to face with Carlos for the first time. He was short, like most of the men here, with leathery skin, a man with an age impossible to guess. He was very, very skinny. Alarmingly skinny. The way his bones poked through his skin was my main concern until I saw his eyes. I cannot accurately describe the way they jolted my heart, blinking rapidly a few times to ward off the strong sunlight. It was as if all the sadness in the world had been boiled down into two deep, condensed, brown pools. There was something so raw, so deep, so hungry and so very human in those eyes. They housed anguish, but not the blind terrified anguish of a moment—the steady, deep, fully conscious anguish of many long years. With a gesture of his gnarled hand, he led us inside.

The first thing I noticed was the smell: body odor, rat and dog urine, and well-fermented garbage. It washed over me as I stepped inside. As I entered, my feet stuck a little to the filthy floor with each step; everything was covered in a layer of grime and grease and filled with all types of trash imaginable. The house was devoid of light, save what entered through the open door. We could hear the rustling of rats and the slow shuffle of his feet as he led us to a place to sit and chat. I don't remember a whole lot of what we talked about, just those burning eyes. He livened up considerably as we talked, but when the time came for us to go, his face fell again. "Don't worry, we'll be back."

We returned regularly in the following months, each visit more or less the same, talking about everything and nothing, the face falling as we passed out the door. However, in our visits, we started noticing little changes in Carlos's house and in himself. One visit, the window was open, the next, there was less trash, and the house was a little more organized. The next, his hair was combed and his face clean and his bed made. Little by little, he was improving his life himself. His dignity was being restored. Just by existing, being here, talking about insignificant things and passing time with him, we showed him he was worthy. By being loved, he could then start to love himself and drastically improve his life and his situation. In his loneliness and pain, he lacked motivation to live, but the simple presence of another gave that back to him. His eyes burn less now, and his health is improving. We accompanied him once to see a doctor, who told us there was nothing specifically wrong. It was just the loneliness and its consequences that had taken such a terrible toll on his body.

Before I left on mission, I was asked by everyone, "What are you going to *do* there?" I always answered with a classic line about presence and dignity, to "be" rather than "do," but in my heart, I hadn't the faintest idea. Why wasn't I going to do something, to build, to change? Now I understand a little better, thanks to Carlos. If we had built him a new house to replace the filthy one he has, would it have motivated him to be clean? If we had built him a new hospital, would it have motivated him to be healthy? Most importantly, would he have felt loved, or would his eyes continue to burn and burn? It is so beautiful; we come with empty hands and give our hands themselves . . . and naturally our hearts go right along with them.

"We think sometimes that poverty is only being hungry, naked and homeless. The poverty of being unwanted, unloved and uncared for is the greatest poverty. We must start in our own homes to remedy this kind of poverty." — *St. Teresa of Calcutta*

Now He Runs a School

Sofia – Senegal

Antoine was born physically handicapped and, because of this, was not deemed worthy to be sent to school like his brothers and sisters. When his mother passed away, his father gave him up, forcing him to live on the street. This is where Antoine met a group of Con-solatio volunteers. Moved by compassion at the sight of Antoine, they brought him to live in our home for several months until they were able to find a place for him to stay and were able to sign him up at Talibou Dabo, Grand Yoff's school for children who are handicapped. Antoine told me that it was during this time living with us that he was able to accept for the first time that he was worthy of love, having been made to believe the opposite for his whole life up to that point. Today, the Antoine I know is in his late 30s. Not only did he finish school but he went on to the university, obtaining higher academic degrees than all his siblings. Now he runs a school for children who are handicapped where he makes sure that every child knows that they have dignity and potential.

Antoine doesn't come by our home very often, but when he does, he never fails to express his thanks. I can tell that he still carries many wounds from his past, but that does not stop him from accomplishing the work he is passionate about. I do not know if the volunteers that loved Antoine first have heard about what he has become today, but his story shows me in a very clear manner the way that presence bears fruit. During our mission (and life!) we can only provide love in the present, and we will never know if it is enough.

The volunteers that encouraged Ahmed's love for reading did not know that he would go on to become a professor in comparative literature at Cheikh Anta Diop University, choosing to continue to live in Arafat in order to never forget his humble beginnings.

The South American volunteers that took time to converse with Jeremie in Spanish never knew that this could lead him to teach this language in high school and volunteer as an educator for street children.

The volunteers who loved the rowdy little Philippe earned a faithful friend who continues to be a weekly regular at our home today. Now in his 30s, Philippe helps coach our boys' soccer team, is always available when we need a handyman, and accompanies us to the island of Mar Loj for camp each summer.

Even though I have spent 14 months in this house, we have friends who have known our community since before I was born! It is such an awesome and undeserved privilege to be a part of such a vast family story!

A Waste of My College Education?

Christine – Romania

There are 10 railroad tracks that run between the Deva train station and a neighborhood in Deva that we visit. I have often felt that these tracks are something like the wardrobe leading to Narnia. As we carefully pick our way over each one, we leave a comfortable world of well-dressed businesspeople and fast-food restaurants and slowly enter another world—a world whose inhabitants live under a dark shadow of deep suffering. Families live in two barracks that were once used as pig stalls; their cracked and peeling doors hide rooms in which every form of abuse has taken place. Relationships between men and women are marked by dominance and a deep lack of respect. The children, half of whom are usually naked, play on slabs of concrete strewn with trash and broken glass, their faces covered in dried snot and dirt. Everyone is used to brutality, and it shows in how the children grab each other by the throats after minor disputes and beat the dogs. The neighborhood is home to about 50 families of Deva's poorest of the poor. It's our most physically and emotionally draining apostolate.

While I've noticed that little by little over the past year the children (and the men!) have been behaving better and better when we come, I was completely blown away last week when I went to visit with Blandine. When we arrived, we played with the kids that came out to greet us as we normally do. Already I was thanking God for how beautifully the children played together

199

and with us. However, I was amazed when two older girls offered to play "school" together. Normally it's *us* that have to come up with the games we play, and then we usually are required to spend 15 minutes trying to keep the kids from fighting because not everyone agrees on what game to play. Yet when the girls suggested playing "school," all the children agreed, and they lined up on a tiny wooden bench outside of one of the barracks. Blandine and I were designated as the children's mothers. Each of us was mother to four or five children, and when the "school day" began we hugged and kissed each of them, telling them to behave and listen to the "teacher." They promised they would and waved as they shouted, "Bye Mommy!" to each of us.

Blandine and I hid behind a little shack to listen to their lesson, and we stared at each other in shock to hear all the children counting in unison in *țigănește*. They listened to everything their "teacher" said, and when we came back to the "school" periodically throughout the lesson to see how they were doing, they would all shout, "Mommy! Mommy!" and run to hug us before taking their seats again on the little bench. After a while, we had to explain that we had to leave for real. We expected tantrums to be thrown and for little fights to break out among them, as we are accustomed to when we say that we have to leave, but they just shouted, "Bye, Mommy!" and lined up for their hugs and kisses before returning to their lesson. They waved with huge grins, shouting, "Bye, Mommy!" as we walked away. We left in astonishment to the sound of their little voices repeating their teacher.

Sometimes when I try to explain what Con-solatio is to people, they don't get it. They don't understand the concept of a volunteer who goes into the poorest neighborhoods of the city—not to bring money or food—but only to bring the presence of Christ. More than one person has hinted (or has said quite plainly) that perhaps taking 14 months out of my "life" (which could have been spent working or earning my law degree) and prolonging starting a family of my own to come to Romania to play "school" with a bunch of poor gypsy children isn't really worth it or is a "waste of my college education." But I've seen the power of simple love and its result is an incomparable and indescribable beauty. It's worth every second that I would have spent making money in the States and every tear I shed being far from my family and my country. I don't go there because it's easy or fun (because sometimes it really ISN'T). I come because I love my little friends so much that I want them to know real, true love—the love of Jesus Christ.

While it may seem insignificant in comparison to fundraising or some other activities, what could be more important than the hours that I take each day to do things like help Alexia with her 4th grade math homework, or to hold Mya for 20 minutes straight because she may not ever be shown affection at home, or to celebrate the 73rd birthday of a man from our church who hadn't had a single visitor before we came?

All It Takes to Go From *"Dek Dyy"* to *"Dek Dii"*

Natalie — Thailand

About a month ago, we scrapped our plans upon being invited to a memorial Mass for John Baptiste, a man from our neighborhood who had helped paint our house, and coincidentally, was one of the few Thai Catholics we've met from our neck of the woods. We went to the Mass with John Baptiste's wife and their two grandsons, Net (five) and Not (three).

The little boys had been to our house to play a few times before, and they were *"dyy"* as the Thais say. It's the word for "naughty and misbehaved," and it resembles a sound you might make upon realizing you've just stepped in dog poop—a strong possibility in our neighborhood. The boys would come and throw toys everywhere, breaking some and trying to make off with others, fighting with the other kids, never cleaning up. I was always struck by the fact that they would rarely make eye contact with us and never spoke. In fact, I have to confess that we referred to them as *dek dyy* (the *dyy* kids) for a long time because they would never answer us when we asked them their names. Net and Not had been living with their dying grandfather and their grandmother. Their mother is in and out of the house—hardly ever around—and their father left long ago. Grandma told us that when Net was a toddler, he was very often left locked in a room by himself all day while Mom was at work. He has huge trust and anxiety issues as a result, and he is very slow in his social development and cognitive learning. He often cries so hard at the gate of school that he throws up, and then Grandma ends up taking him home.

Back to the memorial Mass: Thuy, Marie, and I sat in the front pew of the convent chapel with the two boys and their grandmother. Big mistake. Within minutes of the Mass beginning, the boys were up to their usual antics—on steroids. They were throwing hymnals, punching each other, running onto the altar. It made for a great contrast to the rows of blue-habited sisters, hands perfectly folded, all eyes on us. After a few fruitless attempts to restrain Not and Net, Marie and I each grabbed one and DRAGGED them—now kicking and punching us, and screaming—down the aisle and out the door.

With my arms around Net, pinning his arms to his sides, I plopped him on my lap on a bench outside the convent, turning myself into a human straitjacket. My knee accidentally jabbed into his calf, giving him a dead leg. "Ahh! *Jep*!! Ahh! That hurts!!"

"*Dichan jep caij! Jaij duaj!* Well, my heart hurts! Grandma's does, too!" The two of us struggled together for an hour on that bench, with Marie and Not doing the same right next to us. I periodically flashed to the Tyson-Holyfield fight as Net tried to bite me between bouts of crying, yelling, and whimpering, begging me to let him go. The four of us were quite a sight, I'm sure, for all the passersby. By the end, we were all covered in sweat and tears, but thankfully no blood.

When Net had settled down enough to listen, having nearly exhausted himself, I tried to speak to him. I told him that he's not *dyy*—that he's a good kid who does *dyy* things sometimes. I told him that I want him to be good for his grandma, because I know he's good, but that I love him even when he's acting *dyy*. I kissed him on his pouty-faced, tear-streaked cheek. He quickly wiped it off, but then he ever-so-slowly looked up to make real eye contact with me for the first time as if to ask, "Really?" I think that since he's been branded as *dyy* (probably even before he was kicked out of kindergarten), *dyy* was how he saw himself. It had become his identity. Without any time or energy to say much more, Grandma and Thuy came out of Mass and we all headed home—physically and emotionally drained and glad THAT was over.

Well, well, guess who we happened to see on our way into church Sunday morning, two days later? Yep. Net and Grandma! Oh boy. Grandma told us, "Net said that he is going to be a good boy today. He is going to pray for Grandpa." Against all reason, I invited him to sit with me. Surprisingly, he crawled into my lap, which I took as shy acceptance. I whispered into his ear, "I'm so happy that you're here, and I know that you're going to be good, because you're a good kid, right?" He turned his head just enough to show me a subtle smile, which I took as, *"Phii* Nam, I'm going to try my darndest to restrain all my *dyy* impulses, but sometimes those impulses are just stronger than I am. I'm going to try, though. Really." Sometimes you have to interpret the facial expressions and body language of those strong, silent types.

All things (i.e., his squirmy little boy-ness and his short attention span) considered, Net was impressively good during Mass. He was so proud to pretend he was following along in my *Magnificat*, and he kept looking up at us for approval at how quiet he was being. His hunger for positive attention was almost tangible. We were sure to shower him with praise on the way home. He ate it up. He even spoke to me for the first time: he motioned for me to bend down, pulled an action figure out of his pocket, and whispered, "that's Spiderman." The transformation had begun.

Over the last two months, Thuy, Marie, and I have been privileged witnesses to the transformation of one formerly *dek dyy* discovering his belovedness. Net has been coming to play at our house almost every day now. Over time, he has stopped fighting with the other children. He's now proud to show us that he's *dek dii* (a good kid), sharing with his younger brother and cleaning up after himself (well, most of the time, haha). The day after he introduced me to Spiderman (the moment we officially became friends), he brought me a delicious Thai dessert he'd bought for me with money from Grandma. I almost crumpled with joy as he handed it to me and whispered in my ear, *"Haj Phii. For you."* The mornings I hear his little voice calling, *"Phii* Nam! *Phii* Nam!" from outside our house on his way to school are my favorites. When I open the door, he jumps into my arms and waits for me to kiss him on the cheek so that he can give me one in return. Then he'll jump down to run and catch Grandma and Not. Just like that, he can turn my grumpiest and most sluggish mornings into moments of gratitude and grace.

When he's around, Net often joins me for my hour of adoration. Net came and plopped into my lap one afternoon while I was meditating on the Gospel story about John the Baptist's birth— where all the neighbors are shocked and amazed by his father Zechariah's miraculous regaining of speech. Everyone realizes then that John the Baptist is clearly going to be a BIG DEAL, and they all ask, "What, then, will this child be?" Hugging Net close, I was moved to tears by his own miraculous transformation, and that very question became my prayer for him: as he continues to discover his inherent goodness, what will he become?

A New Ray of Light

Madeleine – Argentina

"Anna," Rosalba calls into the open doorway. Rosalba has another friend for us to meet. There are figures inside the one-room house: a tall woman and a girl, slender, with wide-set eyes and then—half-lit by the sunlight from the open doorway—a woman curled up on the bed with a urinary catheter lying beside her. "Ahh," Rosalba exclaims, as the woman in the bed pushes herself up on her elbows to greet us. Both their eyes fill with tears. Rosalba knew her friend was sick, but she hadn't known how badly.

Rosalba introduces us to the woman in the bed—explains who we are, that we just want to visit. I sit in the chair next to the bed, and it's like this invisible pull draws me to this woman—to her dark, sad eyes, the desperation distorting a face that must have been quite beautiful, dark bangs streaked with new growth of white strands. "What happened? Have you been sick long?" I ask.

"For five months," she tells me, "since my operation. Since then, I have not been able to walk." She rubs her legs, emaciated from disuse.

"Do they hurt?"

"It's like electricity in my legs." She takes morphine for the pain. There are figures of Jesus and Mary on the table next to her bed. I lean closer to her; her eyes are filling with tears. "I just want to walk again. I always liked to do so many things. I worked, I took care of a child who is handicapped. Now my daughter has stopped going to school in order to care for me. I'm so alone. I just pass the day in my bed. I don't like to go outside because I don't like to be seen like this. When I was in the hospital I almost died; I was dead for some minutes. I saw the clouds open but then I came back." The last word is enunciated with a note of misery. We speak low, but I can feel the presence of her 11-year-old daughter Maria sitting a few feet away on the couch. "I think I'm losing my faith," she says, her voice breaking. "I pray and pray, but I think I'm losing my faith." I take her hand and she holds it so tight, her look into my eyes so deep and so desperate—help me. God. What do I even say? Come, Holy Spirit. So, I talk to her softly, and I remind her about who Jesus is. I promise her that she isn't alone, that we are going to be with her. "Thank you," she says.

Since then, we have visited Anna four or five times. Every time, it's the same. She cries so much. She bends over and rubs her legs. "I never passed a Christmas like this," she cried. "There are people who rob, who kill . . ." a note of anger in her voice. Why? After our first encounter she went to the doctor and discovered she has a tumor. But the visits—they're not always about her sickness. Maria, her daughter, is a ray of light. You see that when her mom turns inward again and the darkness threatens to overwhelm, Maria tries to cover the sadness, flashing a smile with her bright teeth and asking, "and in the United States there is a lot of snow on Christmas, right?" Or showing me her reggaeton on her tablet, sharing an earbud, her mom watching with interest. Or asking me how to say things in English. Or teaching me words in their native Paraguayan language of Guarani—drawing her mom into the game.

On one visit, I brought a priest with me; he spoke with Anna for a bit of time. When they were finished, the other volunteer and I drew close again. "Anna wants to make her First Communion," Father Miguel told us.

207

So, we returned later to give Anna her first lesson about the faith. We talked about the Eucharist. It was one of the most beautiful things I have ever done. When we began, Anna complained of a headache, that she hadn't slept. All the same, she was receptive to beginning. Then, little by little, Anna and Maria opened up more and more and asked questions of all kinds and we talked about so many things—confession and Mary and the Trinity. Anna asked me to bring her a rosary. Maria asked us two or three times to show them how to pray the Rosary until finally we taught them to pray it. We prayed the decade of the Annunciation because there was a picture in the catechism book and Maria didn't know the story, so first we talked about how God asked Mary to be the mother of Jesus and how Mary was completely free to say yes or no, how she said yes in trust without knowing all that was going to happen. When Anna's sister and sister-in-law arrived, she announced to them in a strong voice that she is going to receive her First Communion on January 25. Then Anna wanted to take a photo together, and we all sat on the bed to take some photos, and I think it was one of the happiest moments I've ever had.

Suffering: An Invitation

Brittany — Ecuador

There is so much human suffering I have witnessed here. Abuse. Brokenness. Poverty. Injustice. Illness. I do not share with you these stories to depress you but to tell you the importance I have seen of a presence of mercy in our neighborhood.

Father George Kosick defines mercy as, "having a pain in your heart for the pains of another, and taking pains to do something about their pain." That is why Con-solatio exists: to be this work of mercy in the world. That is why I am here, with my community, to be part of this work of mercy, specifically in the *Isla Trinitaria*. When there is mercy, there is hope. Hope that one man, one child, one person can learn to truly love and be loved.

What is the Con-solatio response to this suffering? We try not so much to eradicate the difficult situations as to live the prayer of asking God to change the hearts of the persons amidst their situations. We visit Josue weekly, feed him, pray with him, and surprise him on his birthday. We invited Miguel to watch *Slumdog Millionaire* as a way to educate him on the dangers of the street. We have connected Miguel with a friend of ours willing to come weekly to teach him how to read. We have offered Don Jorge a home at Mother Teresa's House of Peace, but he decided for the moment he will continue living on the street since he is now accustomed to living alone. "Maybe when I am older," he says. So, we continue to greet him in the street and stop for a chat.

We have a strong friendship with Sandra and her partner, Ricardo. We encourage Ricardo to not be afraid but to consider committing himself in matrimony before God to the woman he loves. We bring up the topic of violence in the home and try to educate Brisa's parents on true familial love, which is not based in fear. We have gotten to know Armando's mom and have accompanied her to a family counselor. We have suggested that she pay someone other than her mother to care for the kids, as the boys suffer the most when with her, and we are working on getting the boys to see a psychiatrist.

We are conscious that these little gestures are not a "cure-all" by any means. The mission is much bigger than offering practical solutions. The mission is to love like Christ.

How do I understand suffering?

When there is suffering, my natural tendency is to shy away. It's overwhelming, and I do not always know how to respond. It is hard to look at suffering, but I have learned that suffering is not something to turn away from, but rather to press into. I have learned to not be afraid of the face of suffering. It is rather an invitation.

It is an invitation to offer *Señora* Laura my gentle caresses as she is unconscious, suffering the effects of cancer during her last few days on earth. It is an invitation to go visit *Señora* Magali whose son was murdered the night before and offer to start a novena. It is an invitation to give hugs out generously to all the kids who do not usually get hugs at home. It is an invitation to educate Lucia, whose hands and feet are crippled due to arthritis, that she can offer her suffering to God as a powerful prayer if she offers it in love.

An invitation to spend an hour chatting with Rhamses who comes to our house every other Saturday to bring us breakfast.

He says that we (the Con-solatio community) are his refuge, his place of peace.

Though I will soon go away from this beloved *Isla Trinitaria*, I won't forget the pain in my heart for their pains. I rest assured that our friends will continue being loved. I say "our friends" because they are not only mine but those of the whole community. They will continue the friendships and work of mercy long after I am gone. I have not been alone here. I have not made decisions alone. I have learned by living in community that it is not so important that I be the one to do something or say something good for another, as much as that SOMEBODY does it. I rest assured that SOMEBODY in my community will continue loving and serving here in the *Isla*, and that gives me great comfort as I prepare to leave.

Chapter Ten
And It Was Just the Beginning!

The Most Transformative Truth:
I Myself Was One of the Poorest

Marylouise — Wisconsin

The girl sitting on the airplane from Wisconsin to Vienna 18 months ago wouldn't recognize the one who took that same 11-hour trip back home. I was excited, nervous, full of anticipation in face of all the love I had bursting inside of me that I couldn't wait to give. I felt so rich and ready and inspired! Yet, I cannot deny that on the other hand I was battling the lingering hesitation and my bafflement at the destination code written on my luggage tags, VIE. As I boarded the plane, my mind raced with questions I had heard so many times when describing to others what I was leaving to do. "Vienna? Why Vienna? What kind of poverty and suffering is there? Who needs help there? What will Con-solatio do there?" The questions found their counterparts with physical images of poverty-bloated bellies and bones covered with thin skin and ragged clothing—"poor ones" to whom I yearned to give some of my heart-wealth and who I thought only lived in particular parts of the world in particular living situations.

Then that plane landed, and as God's adventure unfolded, in the midst of so many awe-inspiring experiences, friendships, treasures, and answers, I came to discover the deepest and most transformative truth—I myself was one of the poorest. I needed the community in Vienna to show me my poverty and share with me what it means to be human, to love and to be loved. I, with a poverty-bloated belly and ragged clothes covering my frail bones, didn't know how big my hunger was. I didn't know how much of a beggar I was. I didn't know how painful my thirst was. Then, through the open hearts of those we met, I began to discover the depths of my humanity. I looked into the eyes of my friend, community members, or a complete stranger and discovered my gnawing hunger for peace, joy, understanding, mercy, and love— the gnawing hunger of my humanity. I knelt down and begged again and again for the love and forgiveness of the one standing before me. I discovered my thirst to be understood and accepted.

Packed in this humble discovery is the heart of my presence, of our community's presence in Vienna. Not to stand on the edge, on the outside and minister or organize or problem-solve, but to be invited inside, to embrace, to follow, and in spite of at times excruciating pain, to be united in the humbling poverty and awesome dignity of our humanity. I had nothing to offer those to whom God led me except the ability to be beside them, to share, to be united with them and in that nearness to show them their own awesome dignity as children of God.

What is this poverty that unites? It is an insecurity—not the insecurity of losing a job, not having enough to eat, or not having the opportunity to go to school. Instead, it is an insecurity that could easily lead to madness. It is the insecurity of our deepest human need. It is the insecurity that continually screams out, "Please! Love me!" and the insecurity of waiting for a response. In this insecurity, I, along with those with whom I have found myself united in this poverty, have the opportunity to truly experience for the first time the dignity of the human person—a dignity grounded in a hope that has already been fulfilled by an eternal response: "Yes! I love you!" The fulfillment of hope found in the never-ceasing and ever-consoling presence of Love Himself—a Love that satiates insatiable hunger; a Love that quenches tormenting thirst; a Love that requires dependence and gives eternal Presence; a Love that requires insecurity in order to give peace.

In the end, the echoing cry of love, which is the poverty that unites every one of us, finds its reply within a Presence that doesn't satiate on demand, but expands in order to fill even more, and to expand and fill again. We are merely called, in all our humbling poverty, to let this love expand in and through us, becoming small, radiating signs of hope to those who have not heard His voice or felt His touch by offering our own humble nearness.

Simply to Accept Dinner Invitations

Sofia – Michigan

During the two weeks leading up to my departure from Senegal, I felt like I was dreaming. I was doing many "last things": visiting Mbeubeus (the garbage dump) for the last time, drinking my last bagged water (yes, the H2O comes in little plastic bags in Senegal), playing the *kora* (Senegalese harp) for the last time in the chapel . . . . Amidst all these things, I had the greater realization that life goes on without me. It is a quite humbling thought: the community will get by just fine, our friends will continue their lives of work and school, and new volunteers will take my place.

Amidst all these thoughts, I came across a reflection on one of Jesus' parables which helped me understand the goodbyes I would be saying shortly. The reflection started by presenting the parable of a man who prepares a large feast for no pretext and invites his peers to come and eat. The guests tell him (for various banal reasons) that they cannot come; therefore, the man invites all of those who are poor found on the street to come to the feast together. Why didn't the man's peers come to the feast? Apart from accepting the invitation, a sign of their friendship with the host, they had nothing to gain from coming, nor were they being pressured to accept—the invitation was completely gratuitous. The people living on the street respond differently to this gratuitousness. They know that the invitation is not a promise to end all their problems nor to acquire future comforts; yet, they decide to be present anyway. After the dinner, they return to their regular existence; however, from now on everything has changed for them because of their new friendship with the dinner host.

This reflection reminded me that I did not go to Senegal in order to do great things. I was not there to get all of my friends out of poverty, to find them jobs outside of Mbeubeus, to provide them with healthcare, education, government aid, etc. My mission was to seek to respond to the deepest of human needs: the need to be seen, to be visited and to be loved. I came to accept dinner invitations and to invite others to come to my dinners. In doing this, I had the privilege of becoming an "event" in my friends' and community members' lives, and they became one in mine. I believe that none of us can live the same way as a result.

To Live More Humanly in the States, I Needed Brazil

Michael – Pennsylvania

Another friendship that has opened me up wide over the past few weeks has been with a married couple in their early forties, Lucas and Martha. Lucas was hit by a car last year during Carnival, and their lives changed drastically as they've spent the last year trying to recover—physically, emotionally, financially—together. After over a year of surgeries and treatments, his leg is still mangled, and he can only walk with great difficulty and help from others. Seeing the way that their lives—with all of their projects, plans, and dreams—effectively stopped and now revolve around Lucas' ailment can be heartbreaking, but seeing the way that Martha cares for her husband has been so powerful and important for me over the past months: she gave up everything else and now just spends every day caring for him, giving her life completely to another human being.

There's nothing glorious or dramatic in her life, just changing his sheets and cooking his lunch, being patient when he's lashing out because he feels impotent, sitting with him when he's in pain, laughing with him when he's open to joy. She gets frustrated: one day we just sat outside her house and she hung her head and mumbled over and over, "I can't do it anymore, I can't do it anymore. . ." Yet the next day, she kept doing it. After having traveled thousands of miles with visions of saving the world, of intense, dramatic encounters with the poorest of the poor, I'm finding myself hugely humbled by this woman who does nothing more than care for one other human being, and in so doing is living a fecundity and a love that's opened my eyes to the real, concrete, infinite value of just one human being.

I've been especially struck recently by the fact that, while we started visiting this family to be present to Lucas—who was suffering intense physical pain—it was ultimately his wife who responded to our friendship. It was Martha who smiled hugely or subtly sighed with relief when she saw us in her doorway, who came to our house when she needed a friend, who held onto us and let us into her heart. We came intending to accompany someone suffering physically, visibly, obviously, but in the end, God worked even greater wonders with the person hurting silently at his side, the person nursing a hidden pain, with a heart as mangled and tender and raw as her husband's leg.

This all resonates with my life before Brazil as well—I think of friends in the States who may not have been suffering visibly or obviously, but who were carrying very real and very deep pain and who needed a compassionate presence. That gives me hope. It can be daunting imagining going from my neighborhood here back to my parents' house, from friends who live in serious poverty and are tormented by the relentless threat of violence to friends in med school whose problems can seem trivial by comparison. Yet I know that even if the loved ones I'll see again in a few weeks may not be suffering visibly, that we all carry a wound in our heart, even if it's hidden; we're all crying out for the God of mercy and love, even if we stifle that cry; that we're all called to live compassion, as much in a suburb as in a slum. Maybe I had to go to Brazil to learn all that—to learn how to live more humanly in the States.

I've Tasted the Water! I Cannot Possibly Let It Go!

Savanna – Louisiana

During the last few days, I was really feeling the weight of my departure and a little bit of fear at having to go back home. After months of waking up at 5:30 every morning, washing hundreds of dishes, cleaning dirt and food from the floors, hand washing our clothes each day, sleeping on the floor (with God knows what kind of insects), explaining a simple addition problem for an hour to one of the children, and being fully present to the community, I had discovered a most selfless and deep love here. I was quenched; I had tasted the water! I did not want to let it go!

The moment I got on the train to go to the airport my eyes filled with tears and my heart with sorrow. I could not believe I was actually leaving. So, I finally arrived in Chennai for my first flight, went through security, and quickly boarded the plane. As I was taking my seat on the plane, I sat next to an older Muslim woman whose name was Derina Amma. She looked at me and noticed I had been crying, and she touched her cheeks and said, "Crying?"

She could hardly speak any English, so I just shook my head and said, "Yes, because I am leaving India." At this moment, she also began to cry and told me with very broken English that her husband has cancer and has only 20 days to live. After telling me this, I could feel the pain in her heart, and I just held her arm and we sat there in silence grieving together.

I then noticed that she had her prayer beads in her hand, so I asked her if she was praying. She said yes, so I then asked if I could also pray with her. She said yes and then proceeded to chant her prayers to Allah, while I was quietly offering my prayers to the Lord for her and her husband.

This particular moment was such an affirmation of my time in India. Derina Amma was a great last driving force for me to continue to live this life of love and compassion with my newly fashioned heart, to seek out those who are lonely, isolated, suffering, and spiritually impoverished everywhere I go.

With My Newly Fashioned Gaze

Veronica — Michigan

How strange it is to be writing this final letter to you from my home in Sterling Heights, Michigan, with snow falling outside. How strange it is not to hear any of the normal noises of life in the *Ensenada*, which include many things: moto-taxis speeding by, children running home from school, the music that is blared through loudspeakers in the neighborhood market. Over 15 months ago, as I began my mission, this constant noise bothered me, especially during my time in adoration, the only hour of the day when I could (almost) be guaranteed no interruptions. However, as time went by, even the noise became dear to me, as it was something particular to my neighborhood, to my life, and to my friends. How strange it is not to be speaking Spanish from morning to night and to be going to Masses said in English again. How strange it is not to have friends walking through the door of my house at any hour of the day to ask a favor, to pour out their hearts over a cup of tea, or simply to drop in for a moment because they were passing by and saw the lights on.

I never thought I could experience culture shock coming into my own country, but that is exactly how I would describe my arrival in Detroit on December 15. I have been putting off writing this letter since then, because I was afraid. The time I spent in Lima was so beautiful, and my departure was so moving and difficult that I was afraid of my inability to summarize my

224

mission and to express to you everything that God did during my time there.

I received many blessings, words of advice, prayers and requests during my going-away party, as I hugged my friends for the last time and cried in their arms, thanking God for their friendships. However, the phrase that I heard from almost everyone and that still rings in my ears was this: *"No te olvides de nosotros. Don't forget about us!"* This cry that was said through tears, by people whom I had visited multiple times throughout the course of my mission, whom I had welcomed into our own home, and with whom I had shared both moments of great pain and joy, has so much depth and meaning behind it. It is a cry that expresses their desire to be recognized, their need to be loved, and their right to have their dignity and humanity respected. They didn't tell me not to leave, for they understand that the departure is part of our mission, but instead they begged for this recognition: to not be forgotten after I had left their country. The ironic thing is that this was my very cry throughout my entire mission, a cry that I directed to Christ every day in the chapel, asking Him to accompany me, for I discovered very early on that it was futile trying to live by my own strength. So, all I can do is turn this cry over to Him, as I begin to adjust to life in the US again, adapting to my new reality, yet never forgetting those whom I have left behind physically and who remain with me in my heart.

I could fill a book with the things that I learned from my mission. A huge lesson has been recognizing His mercy. From the beginning, my weaknesses and failings were blatantly obvious through the challenges I faced, but Christ never left me. He remained there in the chapel. He showed Himself in the faces of my friends, who would lift me up with their smiles and generosity when I least deserved it. So, I was extremely happy when I heard that Pope Francis had announced a year of mercy, which would begin just as I was leaving Peru. My mission, then, is only just beginning and I have so much more to learn this year and for the rest of my life.

I began this letter by pointing out how strange it is to be back. However, one thing that is not strange, one thing that has remained constant and thus is my greatest comfort, is that I can still go to Mass and Adoration in my parish here and encounter the same Person Who accompanied me throughout my mission. He opened my eyes to His Presence in our reality through so many faces in Peru, and my work here will be the same: to seek that Presence in my friends and family here. In fact, Christ's love has already shown itself to me in so many ways since my arrival: through my family and their patience as my moods change from excitement at being at "home" to homesickness at being away from "home"; through my parish priests and the parish secretary, who gave me a warm greeting after the first Mass I attended back at my church; through a friend who has been through a similar experience and offered to sit and listen to my stories; and through countless others who have opened their arms to embrace and receive me since my return. I don't know yet what Christ has in store for me next as I begin my job hunt, but I pray that with my new gaze gained from this experience, I can live life more fully each day.

More Than Just a Joyful Homecoming

Charlotte — Alabama

One of the greatest things that has totally befuddled me and delighted me since my first encounter with Con-solatio is the sensation of feeling overwhelmingly content and welcome in the midst of foreign lands and people. When I stumbled into a house of French people in the middle of a Brooklyn housing project in March of 2010, I felt truly "in place" for the first time in my life. Six months later, five unknown faces barreled toward me with arms opened wide in the Lima airport and immediately took me on as their sister. Over the course of 18 months, the streets of a smelly yet colorful Peruvian neighborhood became my beloved home and its faces my heartbeat. Three weeks ago, it happened again as I returned to Brooklyn for Alumni Weekend along with nine other former volunteers. Even though I had only formerly met a few of them, they all seemed to be soul friends.

Since I was in Latin America for the better portion of two years, I fell into the trap of limiting Con-solatio to foreign territory. However, on Sunday afternoon, I think my heart finally landed stateside again. After Father Peter celebrated a beautiful Mass, we all gathered in the back courtyard along with several friends from New York for an afternoon full of food, song, dance, children playing, and good conversation. As I contently sat in the midst of a scene that seemed all too familiar, it dawned on me that I was not in Lima, Peru, but in Brooklyn, New York, amongst my fellow Americans.

Nevertheless, it seems absurd and even a bit inhumane to limit my heart's contentment to a few geographical spots or even people, for that matter. Con-solatio proposes totally the contrary: living daily life open to receiving and sharing love. As I laughed and swapped stories with the other volunteers about lessons we learned during our missions, such as the dignity and care shown through a properly set table, whole-heartedly dancing to foreign music for the sake of your friend's birthday, or listening to the same story from the lady on the corner biweekly, St. Teresa of Calcutta's words rang loud and clear, "Don't look for big things, but do small things with great love." For me, Alumni Weekend was not only a joyful homecoming but moreover, a reminder to be faithful to what I have received from Con-solatio in the present moment, in the place where I am, with the people I encounter.

The Philippines Was Just the Beginning

Julian – Maryland

After my return from my mission in the Philippines, my life took a 180-degree turn as I started medical school. I thought nothing would ever compare to the suffering and the poverty I saw in the slums of the Philippines.

As a third-year medical student I get to work in different hospitals in Brooklyn. I will never forget one of my dying patients who suffered tremendously. Anna-Maria was an elderly woman with pneumonia and end-stage renal failure. She only had a few days left to live. Even though she was dying, I never saw any friends or family visit her. I was so saddened by her situation that one afternoon I felt compelled to be by her side and simply hold her hand for a few minutes as she struggled to stay alive. She had no one else to accompany her. This would be the last time I saw her, since she died that night.

Unfortunately, the loneliness and suffering I have seen working in inner city hospitals in Brooklyn is far greater than anything I experienced during my mission in the Philippines. I will never forget seeing hundreds of the loneliest and most depressed people in a psychiatric ward. It is so heartbreaking! Only now can I begin to understand why St. Teresa of Calcutta called New York City the poorest and loneliest city in the world. For me, the Con-solatio mission of compassion didn't end when I left the Philippines; rather, it is just beginning.

Beyond the "You Scratch My Back, I'll Scratch Yours" Mentality

Kari — New York

The shelter-in-place order went into effect in New York on March 22. That same evening, I received an email saying I could start working the next day at 9 a.m. It was a big time of uncertainty as we entered into this new reality of the spreading of the coronavirus and I entered into a new job. However, I was certain of one thing: it was exactly where the Lord wanted me to be.

The interview process itself had been so providential. After speaking with some of my mentors, we decided it would be a good moment to begin applying for jobs in hopes of being hired prior to returning to the US. I had applied to approximately 18–20 jobs. I only heard back from one. At the end of the first round, the HR recruiter said that the next step would be an in-person interview, so I immediately dismissed the possibility of being called. About three weeks later, I received an email requesting, much to my surprise, a virtual interview. My last week in Ecuador, I was offered the position and told which paperwork I would need to submit for the onboarding process. There were a few hiccups along the way, but I managed to get everything on my end submitted before organizations started closing down. Thus, when I received that email asking to start the next day, I knew the Lord had something in store. It was the only employer that responded to my application, an exception was made in the interview process, and Providence would allow me to submit my paperwork before things like registrars' offices were closed.

I was hired to put together workshops on a variety of health topics and to deliver them to the community. My reality is a different one. I fought it a lot the first week because I wanted to do what I was hired to do and couldn't see that I was being asked to be present in a different situation, that of packing bags of food for seniors and those who can't afford food for their families in this crisis. Each week I am amazed at the number of people that show up for food, and it breaks my heart that we run out of bags every time. This past week, people started getting in line at 4 a.m., and by the time we started handing out food at 9:15, we had over 1,000 people waiting. Many of these people are immigrants from Latin America who have lost their jobs in construction companies or restaurants. As time goes on, we see the number of people seeking help in our food pantries and at the "pop-ups" increase as another consequence of this pandemic.

My team reminds me a lot of a Con-solatio community, since it is made up of a Jamaican; a Lebanese; a native New Yorker; a Vietnamese; a woman from the Dominican Republic; and yours truly, the girl from the Midwest that can't wait to wear her cowboy boots to work one day. We are all driven by our desire to serve the community, and I immediately felt like I had been welcomed into a family. This and the work ethic I learned from our dear friends in Ecuador are what keep me going as fatigue starts to kick in after weeks of intense labor.

Since all of us wear masks at work, I am left to contemplate the gaze of each one of them. I barely know them, yet their eyes have become very revealing. I can tell when my boss is tired or stressed about something or when others really wish they could be somewhere else. It is by contemplating their gazes that I made a new friend, Caroline. At first, there was something that drew me to her. She is one of our volunteers and comes from a South American country, so I thought it was perhaps a deep spirituality and the Latino culture that I miss so much that made me want to be her friend. Later, I came to realize that what drew me to her in her gaze was her suffering.

As I got to know Caroline and learned how much she is going through, I immediately realized that being present and being with people in their darkest times isn't needed just in the slums, but especially here in the city that St. Teresa of Calcutta once said was the loneliest city she knew.

Caroline began to tell me that she was looking for rooms to rent and was hoping to go see them one week. That week, we finished packing the bags and I offered to take her to look at the rooms. She was so thankful and moved that somebody would drive her to look at two rooms 15 minutes away from where we were. We arrived and she planned on going to see them by herself and when I offered to go with her, she almost burst into tears. She couldn't believe that somebody would care enough to go with her. She couldn't believe anyone would ever be so nice to her. I told her I believed it was a normal thing to do. She reminded me that here, it is not normal. Her words cut me deep because I realized that she, like many other Americans, is wounded by our culture. I came face to face with a sad reality of my own country: it is rare to find someone who genuinely cares and is willing to help in a time of need. I am thankful for our new friendship, which goes much further than the superficial "doing the right thing" or "you scratch my back, I'll scratch yours" mentalities that usually run rampant.

A Tiny Crack to Achieve a Flood

Natalie — Washington, DC

Con-solatio cultivates a greater openness to those around us and to the invitations of the moment. With this increase in awareness and receptivity, I find myself surprised by and rejoicing a whole lot more, now that I am back home in the US.

A few weeks ago, just as I was getting off the bus to meet a friend in downtown DC, she called to tell me that she was running an hour late. A little annoyed, I started to think about how I would "kill" the hour. Peruse the used book store? Buy a snack in CVS and eat it in the park? As I started to get sucked into my own head and my own plans, a voice a few feet away broke me out of it, "Hello, sir . . . hello, ma'am . . . hello, sir . . . hello, ma'am . . ." It was a homeless man sitting against a sign in front of CVS. I approached him to respond to his litany of greetings, really just to acknowledge his presence. The last thing I had anticipated for that hour was to share it and a Kit-Kat bar with a homeless man. He told me about his job interview preparation meetings the coming week, gifting me with his excitement about his dreams of a life turnaround. He thanked me for stopping to talk; he said no one else in the last four hours had even looked at him. The next week when I walked down that same street, he jumped up like a child and ran to tell me that his meetings went well. Don't we all need someone to share our good news with? Now that stretch of the street is a little more human for me, because I have a friend there.

My 18 months in Thailand taught me that God only needs a tiny crack in the dam to achieve a flood. If we open the door just a sliver, if we meekly whisper a "yes," God will surprise us by taking our five loaves and two fish to feed a crowd—us included.

Acknowledgements

...And so the voyage now becomes yours! The faces, stories, and hearts that have filled these pages invite you to carry on their mission. May you be graced with becoming a loving, unconditional presence to those who surround you. Such a journey, however, is not for lone travelers! The voyage we embarked on with this book was certainly not! We would like to express our immense gratitude to those who have helped shape and give birth to this adventure.

First, we thank our guides—the young Con-solatio volunteers who have led us into some of their most treasured friendships and sacred spaces. We are grateful not only to those who are published here—thank you for your consent!—but to all 120 volunteers who have served around the world since 2005. Through their radical gift of self, we have received the immeasurable gift of meeting thousands of people in their deep sufferings and exquisite beauties. We thank each one of our friends, our masters, for allowing us into their lives and showing us a more intricate and expansive love for life and God.

While our volunteers come and go, the presence of our partner communities remains constant. For this, we are eternally grateful! Thank you to our 18 partner houses in Argentina, Brazil, Chile, Costa Rica, Cuba, Ecuador, El Salvador, Greece, Honduras, India, Italy, Japan, Peru, Philippines, Romania, Senegal, Thailand,

and Uruguay. Thank you for opening your doors and inviting our young volunteers to walk their own paths toward God.

None of this would be possible, however, without the unwavering support of our benefactors. We are filled with immense gratitude toward each person who has sponsored a volunteer; supported various projects in Brooklyn or abroad; and shared generously their money, time, or prayer with us. Thank you for revealing over and over again the miracle of God's Providence!

An enormous thank you goes next to those who have made it possible for these stories to be shared with you. Thank you to our proofreaders, Mara Wickett, Virginia Lichocki, Robert Kustusch, Kathryn Pickens, Sofia Piecuch, and Maura Logue who so generously dedicated their time to helping edit this book. Thank you to our longtime friend, Matthew Sutton, for writing the Foreword and assisting us in the process. Thank you to Rita A. Simmonds, Joe Campo, Laura R. Feola, and Rev. Peter J. Purpura for their words of praise. Thank you to Erin O'Connell for her immense dedication and time given to illustrating the faces of our friends. Thank you heartily to Anna Flournoy, whose hard work and passion made the dream of this book come true.

Lastly, we thank YOU, who have dared the voyage and given yourself to these people and stories. May your life continue to be transformed by God's abiding Presence.

Country and Volunteer Index